To my niece Jessie,
who opened up the door to neurodiversity for all of our family.

About me

My love of cooking started at 10 years of age, I grew up in Dublin and trained in Dublin College of Catering and qualified as a chef. This was my ticket to see the world so I went travelling and I worked with some amazing chefs. I now live in Cookstown Co Tyrone with my Hubby Mark and five boys aged between 14- 22. I have also worked as a Class room assistant with children with Special Educational Needs but am working full time on my business now.

Recently I went back to Loughry College Cookstown and did a degree in Food Technology and a Post Grad in Business Communication. As part of my course I had to carry out a Project on Change Management around the topic of healthy eating with some community groups. The results of this highlighted many people especially parents had a lack of knowledge about nutrition, cooking and budgeting and due to time restraints were depending on highly ultra-processed foods and expensive takeaways to feed their families. Ultra-processed foods contain sugars, starches and additives and are associated with higher risks of obesity, heart disease stroke, diabetes and cancer. Some of the most commonly ultra-processed foods eaten in the UK include industrialised bread, pre-packaged meals, pre-prepared frozen meals, cereal, reconstituted meat products such as sausages, crisps, chocolate, soft drinks, tinned soups, ice-cream and chicken nuggets. (3)
Due to my background in cooking and what I learned during my degree, I felt that this was an area that I could help people with. My younger sister Shaunna created my branding and logo and together we came up with the idea of WYSEBITES (What You Should Eat) in 2019.

Joanna

At WYSEBITES we facilitate cookery and healthy eating workshops and food demos in schools, colleges and community groups throughout Northern Ireland.

We work with adults and children of all ages and abilities to help people to improve their health and wellbeing through cookery. We also work with children and adults who have physical disabilities and impairments, mental health illnesses, Autistic and ADHD children and young adults and their parents/carers.

At our workshops we encourage everyone regardless of their ability to take part and we incorporate equipment and tools to ensure that we are inclusive of everybody.

This year (2023) WYSEBITES are delighted to have won an award from FSB for Diversity and Inclusion and are proud to have achieved this. We love teaching people how to shop, budget, prepare and cook healthier food for themselves and their families to improve their health and well-being.

Over the last 3 ½ years we have been on a journey. Before COVID lockdowns we started off teaching men how to cook! We then helped older peoples groups, sports clubs and schools. This was where we were introduced to many children with food aversions and this was where our Food Sensory programmes came about.

I love a challenge as one of my sons was a fussy eater as a child and was aware of how stressful mealtimes could be. I spent a lot of time coming up with ways to disguise his fruits and vegetables! Thankfully he is a fully grown man with a great appetite now. This inspired me to produce this book and to share some of our delicious tried and tested recipes that will allow you and your family and friends to enjoy cooking together to prepare healthy versions of all your family favourites foods.

What we do...

ADULT CLASSES

The latest data shows that one in four adults (27%) and around one in 16 children (6%) are living with obesity in Northern Ireland. Obesity increases the risk of developing chronic disease, such as colon cancer, high blood pressure, or type 2 diabetes, and is linked to substantial direct and indirect costs – estimated to be of the order of £370 million in Northern Ireland in 2009(20) Using our recipes and tips and advice we aim to educate men and women who want to improve their own and their family's health and wellbeing. We do this privately or in local community groups and organisations and our Adult cooking classes are always a great success.

CHILDREN WORKSHOPS

We love our children's cooking/baking workshops. Here we encourage children to get involved with cooking from an early age. Research shows that there are many benefits for cooking with children. When my children where young we always cooked together and they now are quite independent and confident in the kitchen and often make dinner for us all! Children learn by tasting, touching, feeling, smelling, observing, reading recipes and listening. It also important that children get used to the smell of food when it is cooking so they can link the smell with the food they will eat. (1)

Weighing, measuring and counting can help with their mathematical skills. The processes and changes that takes place during cooking can help children understand the science behind it. Cooking is also great for developing their fine motor and hand-eye coordination skills for example when rolling, squeezing and spreading. Cooking also helps to develop their tastes and encourages them to be more adventurous and to have a varied palette. It can help children develop their creativity and allow them to express themselves while building their confidence, self-esteem and a sense of self-worth as they celebrate their work and feel a sense of pride.

Testimonials...

"Joanna provides a truly amazing program that many children with sensory issues surrounding food would benefit so much from. The program we personally had experience with was so positive. It helped my little boy venture out into trying new foods. He had a diet which was majorly restrictive from 2 years of age up until 6 years which overall impacted his health. He only drank milk but this programme he did in his Learning Support Unit changed that. It took some time but it worked so well and he went from feeling the food to eventually trying it and enjoying it. We now have a little one who is trying all types of food and I as his Mum am truly excited to shop for food - Thanks Joanna x"

"The school have really appreciated the programme; the children have enjoyed this programme and we are really glad to see an improvement in 'X' trying some foods"

1 young person is attending CAHMS and dietician due to food refusal issues school had requested support due to exhaustion in school and concern about refusal to eat at break times re: wellbeing. Since starting this programme, the young person has tried 3 new foods and during the final session with his parent and sibling present he ate a slice of pizza.

"It was a great opportunity for parents and children to hear key messages about healthy eating in a fun and informal way.
Joanna provided a range of fruit and vegetables for children to try. She also showed how to make sandwiches and snacks more fun and appealing to children. I hope that the parents and children will try out some of the ideas at home."

Contents

CHAPTER

01

Food Aversions & Food Sensory

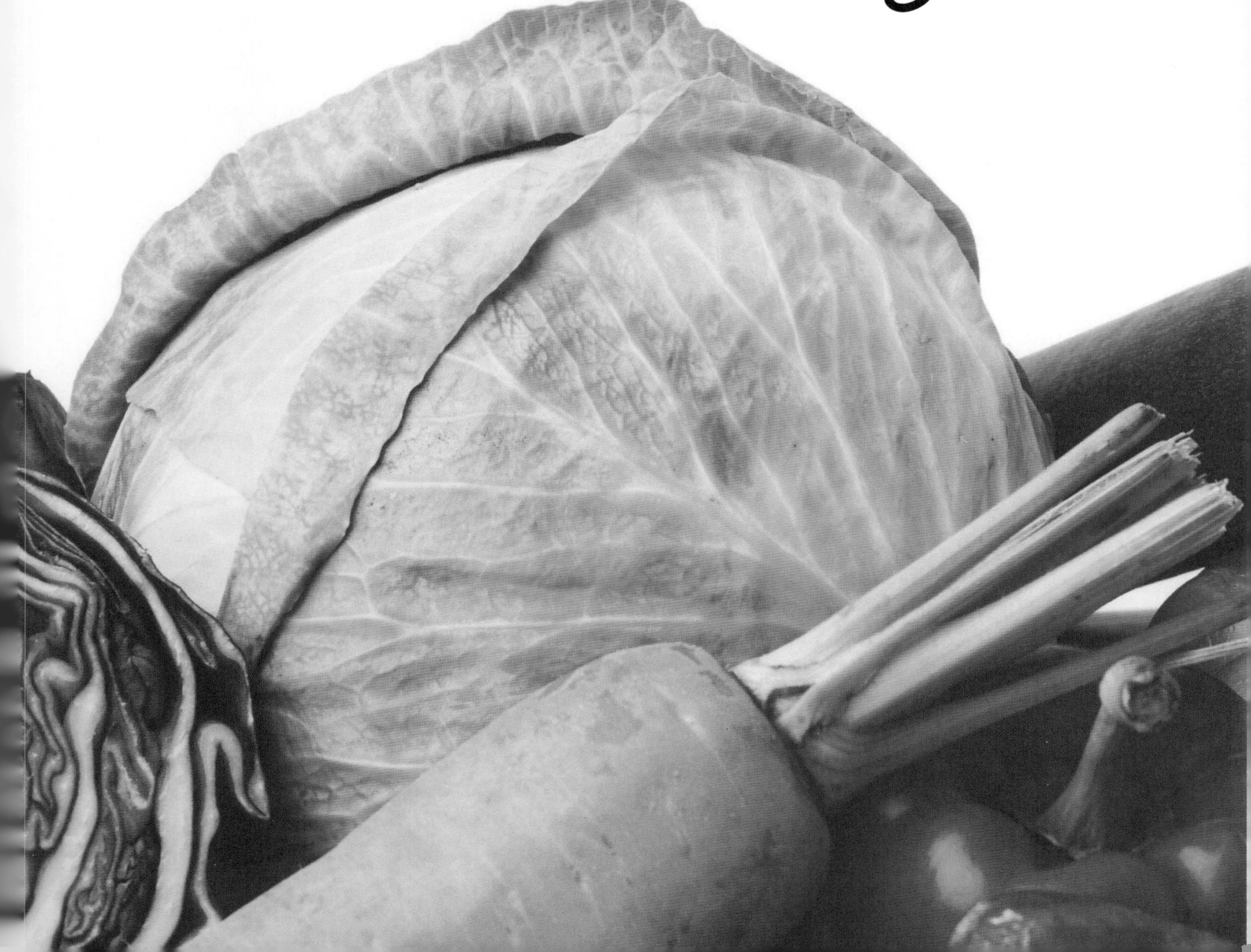

FOOD SENSORY WORKSHOPS

Recent research by the Department of Health (DOH) shows that almost 1 in every 20 school age children in Northern Ireland has been diagnosed with Autism. This is 4.5% of the school aged population and has trebled in a decade (17).

Autistic children are five times more likely to have challenges with meal times such as limited food choices, rituals around their eating behaviours and meal related tantrums (18) This is known as Food Sensory Aversion and it causes children to refuse to eat because of their sensory experience of that food. This can be described as a sensory overreaction to particular types of food. This is often labelled as fussy eating or extreme picky eating but these children can actually stop eating because it's so unpleasant. The taste, smell, texture and temperature of the food can heighten their sensory issues which can result in them refusing to take a bite, spit out the food, gag or vomit during mealtimes. This can make mealtimes very challenging for the child and for parents this can be stressful, isolating and extremely frustrating and can lead to negative feelings and attitudes towards mealtimes and family routines.

At WYSEBITES we have quite a number of children with food aversions at our classes and we are always inclusive to their needs. Research has shown that messy play or any activity where the child interacts with food in a stress-free way seems to help fussy children. Harris and Shea (2018)

This is evident in our Food Sensory Programme that we run for children in schools and children's groups or privately with parents. We have had many success stories and lots of positive feedback from parents, teachers, and group leaders who can see the positive changes to children due to our programmes.

Through these workshops we desensitise children through touch, and play as research has shown that this often helps the child to cope with the different textures in the food and this can help with tasting (4)We do this in a fun relaxed environment with no stresses, introducing children to texture, smell and taste, using child friendly equipment and creating a fun, relaxed environment with no judgement.

We build up confidence and self-esteem in the children allowing them to make their own choices so they can create their own healthier versions of their 'safe foods'.

'Safe Foods' are foods that children with Food Sensory Aversions tend to eat repeatedly eat at every mealtime and becomes part of their routine. However, these 'safe foods' can often be ultra-processed foods containing high amounts of saturated fats, salt and sugar with very little nutritional value. (3)

One of the major concerns of sensory food aversion and picky eating is that this can lead to serious health concerns and have long-term effects on the child's health. Nutrition is central to health, and children's diet can be an important influence on their health now and in the future. Good nutrition in childhood can therefore help protect against chronic diseases in later life.

Changing children and young adults' relationships and behaviours with food is one of our goals at WYSEBITES in order to improve their health and wellbeing for the future.

Practical tips for parents of children with food aversions...

Don't force feed a child

Try give small portions at each meal

Try offering finger foods

Avoid giving squashes and milk before meal times as this can fill them up

Avoid giving snacks to close to mealtimes

Create a calm and relaxed environment at meal times., children can sense stress.

Use brightly coloured dishes and cutlery

Sit together and enjoy your meals together

Lead by example and be wary of your reactions and expressions of food that you do not like as your child will pick up on this

It may take up to 10 times for your child to taste a new food. Don't give up!

Eating Disorders

According to research it is increasingly recognised that autistic individuals are at risk of developing eating disorders such as AFRID, Anorexia nervosa, or Bulimia Nervosa. Almost 10,000 children and young people in the UK have started treatment for eating disorders and there is a record demand for treatment this year(NHS 2023)

Some of these eating disorders may include:

Anorexia - an eating disorder where you feel a need to keep your weight as low as possible.

Bulimia **nervosa -** losing control over how much you eat and then taking drastic action to not put on weight.

AFRID - Avoidant/Restrictive Food Intake Disorder

Pica - is where a child might eat non-food or non-nutritional substances persistently. These substances may include, dirt, soap, chalk sand ice and hair.

Hyperphagia - medical name for Prader-Willi syndrome where the patient develops an increased appetite and eats an excessive amount of food if they have the opportunity. Can cause young adults to develop serious obesity- related conditions. (21)

If you are concerned about your child's eating habits speak to your GP or a Health professional. The NHS website has lots of information to help you too and point you in the right direction.

Children are quite resilient and will not harm themselves if they don't eat enough for a few days. If the problem continues and your child's weight and growth are affected, ask your doctor to refer you to a paediatric dietitian for further advice.

We help parents too!

At WYSEBITES we feel it is extremely important that we educate the parents and carers too. We run workshops, classes and demos to educate parents about the benefits of healthy food and to give them the skills to improve the health and well-being of their families.

Most importantly we encourage them to cook with their children to recreate healthier versions of their favourite foods to create positive behaviours towards food and eating.

Research shows that children who are fed home cooked foods are more likely to eat a wider range of fruit and vegetables later in childhood and life and that people who eat home-cooked meals, on a regular basis, tend to be happier and healthier and consume less sugar and processed foods (5).

Our recipes use easy to follow step by step instructions and are really delicious to eat using basic foods that can be bought in the local supermarket or shop. Using fruit and vegetables as part of our programme has been a successful way to encourage children to try new foods, while getting the benefits from eating their 5 a day.

There is nothing better than spending quality time and passing on your family traditions to your children when you spend time with them in the kitchen and it's a great way to help siblings build stronger relationships by communicating and cooperating with each other (though they will still fight over something silly!)

Lastly cooking is all about fun for both the child and adult so why not start cooking with your children today and create some wonderful memories (2)

This cookery book has lots of our tried and tested recipes that we have used in our workshops and that contain many of the components of the EATWELL GUIDE (NHS) which is a policy tool used to define government recommendations on eating healthily and achieving a balanced diet.

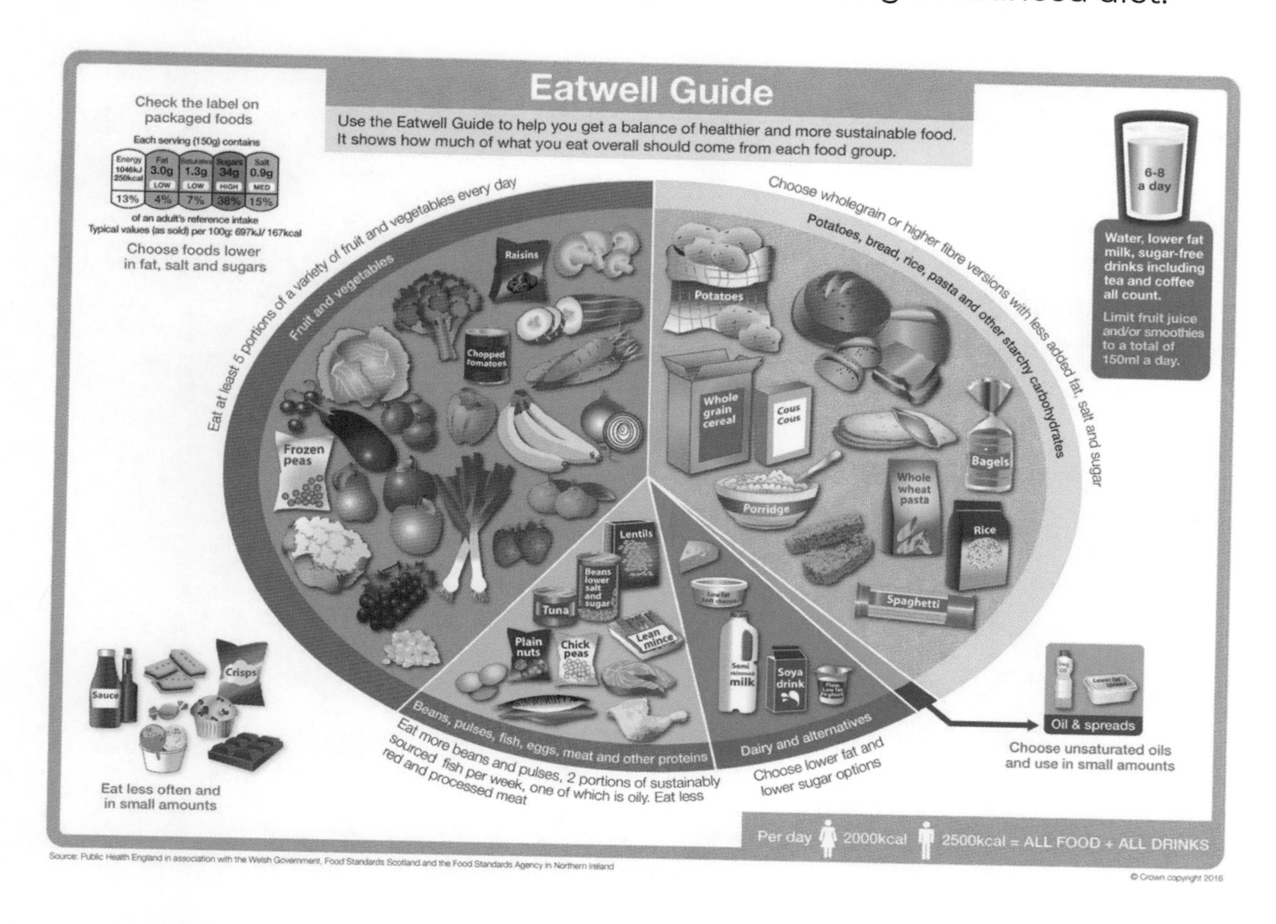

Food Groups

- Fruit and vegetables
- Potatoes, bread, rice, pasta and other starchy carbohydrates
- Dairy and alternatives
- Beans, pulses, fish, eggs, meat and other proteins
- Oils and spreads

We suggest that parents get children involved with shopping, washing up and preparing food to. Children love getting involved and should be encouraged from an early age.

Taking away the choice of unhealthy snacks such as biscuits, crisps and bars and offering healthier snacks such as fruit, crackers, cheeses, rice cakes etc may help encourage your child to make healthier choices.

Food essentials...

Some of our store cupboard essentials that we recommend buying when you are shopping include:

Tinned tomatoes, passata, tomato puree, wholemeal pasta, wholemeal rice, Wholegrain or wholemeal bread, wholegrain pitta breads, tinned items such as beans, lentils, mixed beans, chick peas, low salt stock cubes, dried herbs and spices. We also use eggs, butter, olive oil, extra virgin olive oil, fresh fruit and vegetables, cheese and chicken, fresh or frozen fish, low fat mince and beef and bacon.

Recommended equipment

Oven trays, hand held food blender, hand held food mixer, grater, plastic juice squeezer, colander, baking bowls, sieves, digital scales, measuring cups and spoons, plastic measuring jugs, cake tins, silicone liners for baking, colour coded chopping boards, kitchen utensils like slotted spoons and ladles. Rolling pins, aprons, cutters and wooden spoons.

Tips used during our workshops to ensure good food hygiene...

Always wash your hands

Tie hair back

Wear an apron

Keep raw and cooked foods separate when storing and using

If possible use colour coded chopping boards

Always cook or reheat food to 75°C, using a food thermometer to check core temperature

Only reheat cooked food once for eg, fried rice. Do not reheat again as this can cause food poisoning

Cover and store food in fridge as soon as it cools down. Do not leave cooked food in an oven or microwave over night. Chilling food stops the growth of bacteria

Make sure frozen food such as meat or cooked dishes are fully thawed out before cooking. Thaw in fridge

Check use by dates (eg milk, packet ham) and best before dates (tinned food)

Change kitchen cloths and towels daily. Wash at 60°C

Clean out fridges and food cupboards regularly

Clean as you go! (16)

Disclaimer - Please, be careful with knives, don't cook recipes with ingredients you're allergic to, and use your best judgement with raw ingredients. You are responsible to do the necessary research and make appropriate food-handling decisions for you and for your own family

CHAPTER

02

Easy Breakfast, Lunches & Snacks

Easy Breakfast, Lunches & Snacks

The following recipes are some of the ones that children seem to love so why not take some time with your children and try these out for lunches, snacks and weekend brunches with all the family.

Just remember to have plenty of kitchen roll, mops and cloths handy...It's going to get messy!

Try to encourage your children to eat breakfast as research shows that those who do tend to do better in school, they get more fibre and calcium and it improves their memory and attention which they need to learn.

The importance of fibre in children's diets

Fibre can provide various health benefits for your child.

It can help with their digestive systems promoting regular bowel movements and prevent constipation. Many children are constipated due to snacking often instead of eating at regular meal times (8). Constipation is also the most common bowel problem among individuals with autism and about 5 – 30% of children in general experience constipation (22).

Fibre can take a long time to digest keeping the child more active for longer therefore preventing them from over eating. This can help reduce the chances of obesity in childhood. Fibre can also help regulate children's blood sugar levels as it keeps the sugar and insulin levels steady in the body, controlling diabetes. Fibre is also important for reducing cholesterol and can protect your child from heart disease and bowel cancers. Fibre is found in cereals, fruit and vegetables. It is not digested in the body and as it passes through your digestive system, it soaks up water and makes your stools softer(9).

However, to ensure that fibre works well it is important to drink sufficient fluid (12) especially for Autistic children. It is recommended that Children aged 1-4 drink water regularly throughout the day and children aged between 5-11 between 6-8 small glasses of water a day. Older children should drink 6-8 larger glasses a day (14).

We encourage parents to buy wholemeal, wholegrain or high fibre white bread, pasta, rice, flour, bread, pitta bread, bagels and wraps as we use these in our recipes. You will be surprised that no one notices the difference. See table below for guidelines on how much daily fibre is recommended for your child (this does not apply to children under 2).

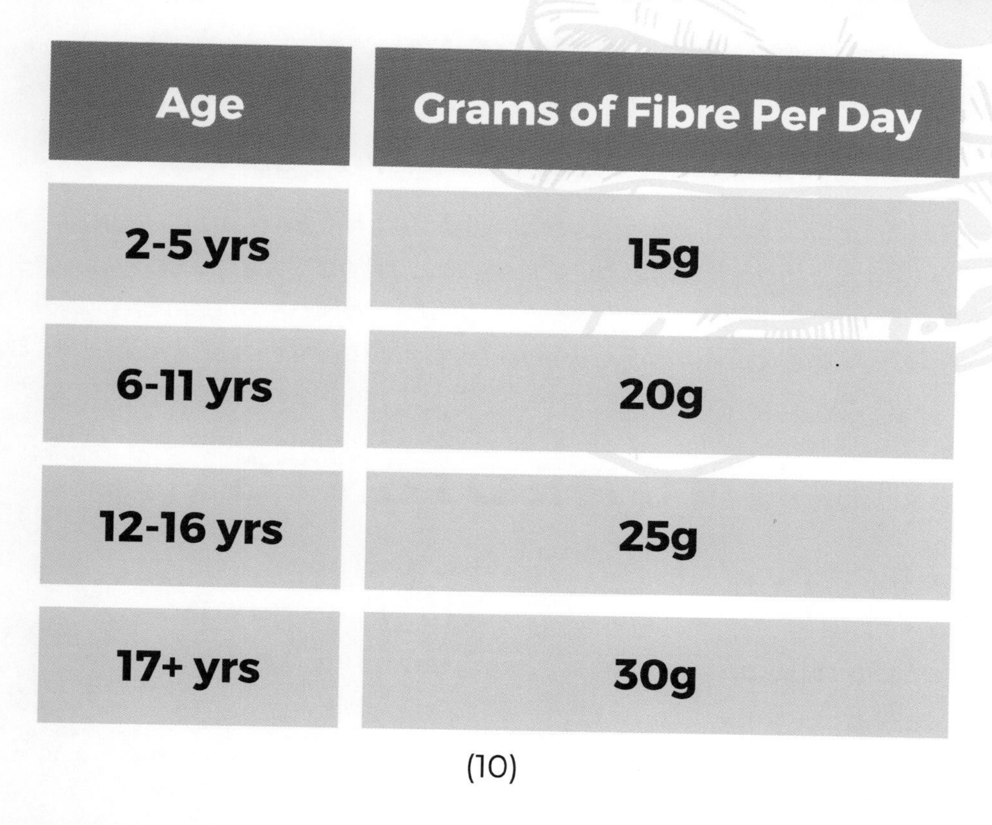

Age	Grams of Fibre Per Day
2-5 yrs	15g
6-11 yrs	20g
12-16 yrs	25g
17+ yrs	30g

(10)

Using whole oats are a great way to start the day as they are a good source of energy, vitamins, minerals, and fibre (10.5)

The following section includes some of our favourite recipes that contain oats.

Apple Oat & Raisin Muffins

Prep - 10 min Cook - 15 min Serves - 6

These are a favourite in my house since my children were small. They are easy to make and high in soluble fibre. You need 2 large bowls, one for wet ingredients and one for dry. These muffins can be used for breakfast or snacks and they last a few days in an airtight container. However they can get crumbly so if you don't like a messy floor make sure they eat off a plate!

INGREDIENTS

- 1 egg
- 6 fl oz of full fat milk
- 4 ½ oz plain flour
- 2 oz castor sugar
- ½ tsp mixed spice
- ½ tsp ground cinnamon
- 6 oz raisins (or grated carrot
- 5 fl oz of sunflower oil
- 3 oz of porridge oats
- 3 tsp baking powder
- ¾ tsp salt
- 1 and a ½ apple. Peeled and cored and chopped

METHOD

- Weigh out all your ingredients
- Add flour, oats, baking powder, sugar and salt to a mixing bowl.
- In a separate bowl, beat egg, milk and oil together.
- Pour the wet mix onto the dry mix
- Add the chopped apple and raisins
- Do not over mix
- Prepare bun cases and add spoonfuls of mixture to each one.
- Bake at 180.oc Gas mark 4 for 15 minutes or until golden brown.

Oat & Banana Pancakes

Prep - 3 min   Cook - 5-6 min   Serves - 1

We make these at our workshops and kids love them. If you have a blender you can blend the mix to make a smooth batter if your child doesn't like lumps!

INGREDIENTS

- 1 egg
- 1 banana
- ½ cup of porridge oats
- Blueberries/strawberries
- Maple syrup/honey
- 1/2 tsp olive oil

METHOD

- Beat the egg into a bowl, add mashed banana and add oats. Mix well.
- Heat a non stick pan and add a knob of butter to melt.
- Divide mix into three and fry in oil until golden brown and then flip and repeat.
- Serve with blueberries and strawberries and a drizzle of maple syrup or honey.

Flapjacks

Prep - 15 min Cook - 40 min Serves - 6

INGREDIENTS

- 175g/6oz butter
- 175g/6oz muscovado sugar
- pinch ground ginger (optional)
- 175g/6oz golden syrup
- 350g/12oz porridge oats
- ½ unwaxed lemon, finely grated zest only (optional)
- Melted chocolate

METHOD

- Preheat the oven to 150°C/130°C Fan/Gas 2 and line a 20cm/8in square baking tin with baking paper.
- Melt the butter in a medium pan over a low heat. Dip a brush in the butter and brush the baking tin with a little bit of it. Add the golden syrup and sugar to the butter and heat gently. Once the sugar is dissolved and the butter is melted, remove the pan from the heat and stir in the porridge oats, lemon zest and ginger.
- Pack the mixture into the baking tin and squash down. Bake in the oven for 40 minutes.
- Once cooked, remove from the oven, leave to cool for 15 minutes, drizzle with chocolate, cool, then turn out on to a chopping board and cut into squares.
- These flapjacks are delicious in a packed lunch or as a grab-and-go breakfast.

Smoothies

Prep - 10 min   Serves - 2

It is important that children eat a variety of fruit In their daily diet. A child sized portion is roughly half of an adults and should fit in the palm of their hand but should be encouraged to gradually increase it to the size of an adults portion(13). It's best to drink juice or smoothies with a meal because this helps reduce harm to your teeth(14).

We always start our workshops with these recipes and continue to introduce the fruits every week to desensitise the children. We get them to hold, smell, feel and in most cases taste the foods. This is nearly always a winner! Children love to use the blender stick, however some children do not like the noise of this.

INGREDIENTS

- 1 x apple
- 1x Kiwi
- 1xBanana
- 4 x Strawberries
- Handful of blueberries
- ¼ freshly chopped pineapple
- Juice of 1 fresh orange
- 1 cup of plain yogurt/low fat Greek
- 1 cup milk (preferably semi skimmed)

METHOD

- Wash fruit and peel if required. Chop fruit up into bite size pieces and put into blender.
- Add yogurt and milk and juice
- Blend until smooth
- Any type of soft fruit, fresh or frozen can be used.

Fruit Kebabs

Prep - 10 min Serves - 2

INGREDIENTS

- Banana
- Strawberry
- Blueberries
- Apple
- Kiwi
- Grapes
- Pears
- Oranges
- Cooking chocolate
- Kebab sticks
- Mini marshmallows

METHOD

- Wash and dry the fruit
- Cut up Fruit into chunks
- Separate on a big platter or chopping board
- Thread the fruit through the skewers
- Add a few marshmallows to the skewers
- Melt chocolate in a heat proof bowl over a saucepan of boiling water until melted
- Drizzle chocolate over fruit kebabs, using a plate to collect the sauce

Prep - 10 min   Cook - 10 min   Serves - 2

INGREDIENTS

- 100g self-raising flour
- 50g wholemeal medium flour
- 1 teaspoon baking powder
- 1 teaspoon sugar
- 1 large free-range egg
- 240 ml semi-skimmed milk
- vanilla extract, optional

METHOD

- Mix all the dry ingredients together in a large bowl. Gradually beat in the egg, then add the milk slowly, whisking well to get as smooth a batter as possible.
- If you're making sweet waffles, grate in the orange zest and add a few drops of vanilla extract
- Get your waffle machine ready. Once it's hot, ladle in the batter mixture and seal, following the machine instructions until your waffles are cooked
- Serve with whatever takes your fancy! Let the kids invent their own!
- Ideas for serving: marshmallows, strawberries, melon, blueberries, Greek yogurt, maple syrup, chocolate spread, peanut butter, bacon

Our Favourite Pancake Recipe

Prep - 5 min Cook - 10 min Serves - 2

INGREDIENTS

- 70g self-raising flour
- 30g wholemeal medium flour
- 50g castor sugar
- 1 large free-range egg
- 4 tbsp milk
- 25g melted butter

METHOD

- Mix all ingredients together to form a thick batter
- Add melted butter in at the end
- Fry spoonfuls in a hot non stick pan.
- Turn over when bubbles appear.
- Serve with Greek yogurt and maple syrup mixed together and drizzle over pancakes.
- Serve with fruit

Healthy Vegetable Sausage Rolls

Prep - 20 min   Cook - 35 min   Serves - 6

INGREDIENTS

- 1 tsp oil
- 4 large mushrooms (washed and chopped finely)
- 1 medium courgette grated
- 1 large carrot, grated
- 1 clove garlic, crushed or finely chopped
- 350g sausage meat
- 1 sheet ready rolled puff pastry
- 1 egg, beaten
- optional: 1/2 tbsp poppy seeds or sesame seeds to decorate

METHOD

- Preheat the oven the 180℃ / 350°F and line a baking tray with greaseproof paper.
- Heat the oil in a frying pan and add in the grated courgette, grated carrot, mushrooms and garlic. Cook on a low heat until the vegetables have softened for about 4 minutes. Don't let them brown, you just want them soft.
- Once the vegetables are cooked, add them to a large bowl along with the sausage meat and mix well.

Continued...

METHOD

- While the mixture is cooling take your sheet of puffed pastry and cut it in half lengthways so that you have two rectangle shaped pieces. Divide the sausage meat mixture into two and spread each piece down the middle of the pastry sheets, leaving a gap of about 1cm either side.
- Roll the pastry over the sausage meat mixture so that the two edges meet. Press down with a fork to seal it.
- Cut the sausage rolls into whatever size you like large or small.
- Place the sausage rolls onto the baking sheet and brush with a little beaten egg. Sprinkle some poppy or sesame seeds on top.
- Cook in the oven for 25-35 minutes (time will depend on the size of the sausage rolls so be sure to check them often from 25 minutes) until golden brown and cooked through.
- Serve immediately with a side salad or some mixed vegetables

Mini Pizza Egg Tortilla Cups

Prep - 15 min   Cook - 15 min   Serves - 4

We use eggs a lot in our recipes as they are really versatile and contain iron, protein, fat vitamins A, D, E and B12. This is a great way to get children involved as they love to break and whisk the eggs and cut up all the ingredients.

Be prepared for some messy tables and floors!

INGREDIENTS

- 4 large tortilla wraps (wholemeal)
- 6 free range eggs
- 2 tbsp milk
- ½ onion diced
- ½ red pepper diced
- ½ green pepper diced
- 6 mushrooms (washed and sliced)
- 8 cherry tomatoes
- 2 oz diced bacon/pepperoni
- 4 oz grated cheese
- Salt and pepper

METHOD

- Using a round 3'inch cutter cut out circles from the tortilla wraps.
- Place each circle inside a greased muffin tin.
- Heat oil in a frying pan and add dice bacon, onion, mushroom, peppers and fry gently for 5 minutes until soft.
- Wash and chop cherry tomatoes in half.
- Beat eggs and milk and seasoning together.

METHOD

- Spoon the bacon and veg mix into each tortilla and pour over egg until ¾ full.
- Add grated cheese and bake in a hot oven 180°C for 15minutes until golden brown ensuring and they are firm.
- Allow to cool before putting into airtight container and storing in the fridge.
- Serve with salad or baked beans.

Pitta Bread Pizza

Prep - 10 min Cook - 5-6 min Serves - 4

Who doesn't like pizza! This recipe is always a favourite even with the pickiest of eaters as they love the process of making their own mini pizza and we introduce fresh pineapple to them, let them grate the cheese and put their own toppings on their pizzas. They are a great quick lunch too.

INGREDIENTS

- 1 tub Passata
- 1 clove garlic
- Oregano
- Basil
- 4 wholemeal pitta bread
- 4 slices of Ham
- Peppers
- Cheddar cheese
- Pepperoni
- Pineapple
- 1 punnet Cherry tomatoes

METHOD

- To Make Tomato Sauce
- Pour passata into a bowl
- Add seasoning and garlic crushed
- Mix well
- To make pitta bread pizza
- Chop ham and pepperoni into small pieces
- Deseed the peppers and chop into small dice

Continued...

METHOD

- Grate cheddar cheese
- Chop Pineapple into dice
- Wash and chop cherry tomatoes
- Put pitta bread onto a flat baking sheet or roasting tray and spread tomato sauce all over it
- Sprinkle grated cheese on top
- Add choice of ingredients
- Add another sprinkle of cheese
- Put into a hot oven 180°C, gas mark 6, for 5-6 minutes

Tortilla Toasties

Prep - 5 min Cook - 10 min Serves - 1

INGREDIENTS

- 2 tortillas
- 1x tbsp passata or our home made tomato sauce recipe.
- 25g sliced cheese, e.g. cheddar, Emmental
- Cooked sliced chicken or ham (optional)
- 1 spring onion, chopped

METHOD

- Prepare the filling: top and tail the spring onion and slice into rings. chop the ham into small pieces.
- Place one of the tortillas in the pan.
- Spread the tomato sauce over the tortilla.
- Arrange the ham, spring onion and cheese over the tortilla.
- Cook for 5 minutes, or until the cheese starts to melt.
- Place the 2nd tortilla on top.
- Flip the tortilla over and cook for 4-5 minutes.
- Cut into slices and serve.

CHAPTER

03

Soups

Soups

Some of our favourite soups at our workshops include chickpeas, lentils, sweet potato and butternut squash. When cooked with other vegetables they give a sweet flavour which children seem to like. It is recommended that children eat 5 portions of fruit and vegetables a day to increase their vitamin and mineral intakes, so making soups is a great way to get them to eat their vegetables as they can be blended.

Many of our parents have told us that their children like them and like the texture and taste. Getting children to wash, peel, chop along with measuring and mixing makes this a really interactive activity that can help with motor skills and they will love to taste what they have made.

Using our homemade bread to dip in the soups also ensures that they are getting plenty of fibre.

Chicken Noodle Soup

Prep - 10 min Cook - 25 min Serves - 4

INGREDIENTS

- 1 boneless chicken breast
- 1 tsp fresh ginger
- 1 clove of garlic
- 50g rice noodles or wheat ones
- 2 tbsp sweetcorn
- 2 Spring onions
- 2-3 sliced mushrooms
- 900 g of chicken or vegetable stock
- Dash of soy sauce.

METHOD

- Cook the chicken breast in the stock with the chopped ginger and garlic
- Bring this up to the boil and allow to simmer for 20 minutes
- When chicken is cooked remove form the pot and shred into pieces and return to pot
- Add noodles, sweetcorn mushrooms, spring onion and soy sauce
- Simmer for 3-4 minutes and divide into bowls, sprinkle over the remainder of spring onion

Roasted Butternut Squash, Sweet Potato & Bacon Soup

Prep - 20 min Cook - 45 min Serves - 4

INGREDIENTS

- 1 butternut squash
- 2 sweet potatoes
- Pack of smoked bacon
- 1 large onion
- 2 sticks of celery
- 1 large carrot
- 2 chicken stock cubes
- 1 pint boiling water
- ½ tsp mixed herbs
- Salt and pepper
- Olive oil

METHOD

- Preheat the oven to 180°C gas mark 5
- Cut the squash in half from top to bottom and scoop out the seeds
- Wash sweet potatoes and cut in half from top to bottom
- Put the squash, sweet potatoes and the garlic clove onto a baking sheet, drizzle with 1 tablespoon of the olive oil sprinkle with herbs and season with salt and pepper
- Roast in the oven until it is nice and soft, 30 to 35 minutes
- Remove from the oven and let cool. When it is cool enough to handle, scoop out the flesh and set aside with the garlic clove
- Meanwhile wash and chop celery and carrots

Continued...

- Chop onion and bacon
- Add these to saucepan and fry with tsp olive oil for 5- 10 mins on medium heat
- When roasted vegetables are ready scope out and add to saucepan with stock
- Bring to the boil and simmer and then puree.
- Serve with our homemade bread recipe!

Sweet Potato and Red Lentil Soup

Prep - 10 min Cook - 40 min Serves - 4

INGREDIENTS

- 1 large onion
- 2 sticks of celery
- 1 large carrot
- 2 large sweet potatoes
- 2 large potatoes
- 2 chicken stock cubes
- 1 ½ pint boiling water
- ½ tsp mixed herbs
- 2 cloves of garlic
- Salt and pepper
- Olive oil
- ¼ cup of red lentils
- Dried mixed herbs

METHOD

- Wash celery and carrots.
- Wash, peel and chop the potatoes.
- Chop onion, carrots and celery into dice.
- Wash and chop and dice the sweet potatoes and potatoes
- Add celery, carrots and onion to a saucepan and fry with tsp olive oil for 5- 10 mins on medium heat.
- Add the chopped potatoes and add stock.
- Add lentils, herbs and stir.
- Bring to the boil and simmer for 30 minutes. Puree and season.
- SServe with our homemade bread recipe!

Leek and Potato Soup

Prep - 10min Cook - 40min Serves - 4

INGREDIENTS

- 2 carrots
- 1 onion
- 3 sticks of celery
- 2 whole leeks
- 6-8 large potatoes
- 2 chicken stock cubes
- Olive oil for frying

METHOD

- Wash vegetables thoroughly. Slice leeks down the middle and run under cold tap to remove all dirt from individual leaves
- Dice vegetables into small cubes. Peel/wash potatoes and dice into big chunks
- Fry onion, carrot and celery on a medium heat for 5 minutes until soft
- Add chopped leeks, cover with lid and fry for further 5- 10 mins on med heat, do not brown
- Add chopped potatoes
- Make 2 pints of stock with boiling water and stock cubes & add to pot
- Bring to the boil and simmer for 25 minutes, be careful it does not stick to pot
- When potatoes are soft, puree soup, or leave whole and add ¼ cup of semi skimmed milk and serve
- Season with salt and pepper to taste
- Serve with our homemade bread recipes!

CHAPTER

04

What's for Dinner?

What's for Dinner?

In this section we have chosen dishes and meals that we know everyone loves. Our recipes show you how to cook simple, nutritious dishes that can be batch cooked, frozen and defrosted, easing the pressures and stresses when asked the dreaded question, "WHATS FOR DINNER?!". Some of these recipes have been tried and tested in our adult and children's workshops and online group family cook-alongs, and parents have been delighted with the results, especially when approved by even the pickiest of eaters. We try to incorporate as many types of vegetables, wholegrains, proteins, animal, plant and dairy products in our recipes. Our recipes use beans, pulses and lentils alongside meat, which is a good source of protein, vitamin B12 and iron. It is recommended that children have one or two portions from this group daily. Our recipes also include starchy foods such as potatoes and wholemeal versions of bread, pasta and rice which are a good source of energy. Children should be offered a wide variety of these foods at every meal.

The inclusion of dairy in our recipes is vital as this food group is important during childhood as it is a good source of calcium, vitamins A and D, protein and fat. Calcium helps children to build strong bones and teeth and for nerve and muscle function. Vitamin D is important to help absorb calcium and therefore plays an important part in strengthening bones.

Our family recipes usually involve everyone in the family to get involved no matter how little they are. These recipes can be used for a quick easy mid-week dinner or a planned weekend occasion.

My niece - the next generation!

Tip: Dairy alternatives can be used in our recipes to suit those with allergens. Nuts also contain protein but it is important that children under five do not eat nuts in case of choking

Baked Chicken Goujons

Prep - 20min Cook - 20min Serves - 6

When making these chicken goujons we place them on a tray, open freeze them, bag them and put them back into the freezer. They can be taken out and defrosted when needed and are a healthy version of children's favourites takeaway meals with 100% chicken and no added preservatives or additives.

INGREDIENTS

- 125g/4½oz fresh fine breadcrumbs
- ½ tsp cayenne pepper (optional)
- salt and pepper, to taste
- 2 tbsp vegetable oil
- 4 boneless and skinless chicken breasts, cut into strips
- 50g/2oz plain flour
- 3 medium free-range eggs, beaten

METHOD

- Preheat the oven to 190°C/375°F/Gas 5. Oil two baking trays with vegetable oil
- Mix the breadcrumbs and cayenne pepper in a shallow bowl. Season with salt and freshly ground black pepper. Place the flour in another shallow bowl
- Dip the chicken pieces in plain flour, then in the beaten egg and finally coat in the breadcrumbs. Shake off the excess and lay the chicken goujons on the oiled baking tray. (The process is easier if you keep one hand clean of egg for dipping the chicken in the flour and breadcrumbs.)

Continued...

- Drizzle the goujons all over with more of the vegetable oil
- Bake in the oven for 30-35 minutes, turning once. Remove from the oven when completely cooked through and golden-brown all over
- Serve the goujons with ketchup, barbecue sauce or in a soft white roll

Garlic Mayonaise

Prep - 5min Serves - 6

INGREDIENTS

- 6 tablespoons low fat mayonnaise
- 2 Tbs of Greek yogurt
- 2 large garlic cloves, pressed
- 1 teaspoon fresh lemon juice
- 1 teaspoon plus 3 tablespoons extra-virgin olive oil

METHOD

- Whisk mayonnaise, garlic, lemon juice and 1 teaspoon oil in small bowl to blend. Season with salt and pepper.
- (Garlic mayonnaise can be made 6 hours ahead. Cover and chill.)

Prep - 5min   Serves - 6

INGREDIENTS

- 1 can good quality chopped tomatoes
- 1 red onion
- 2 cloves garlic
- 2 tbsp fresh coriander
- salt and pepper
- Fresh chilli chopped (optional)

METHOD

- Chop onion finely
- Crush or chop garlic
- Chop coriander
- Add tomatoes and mix all ingredients.
- Season with salt and pepper

Garlic Fries

Prep - 10min Cook - 25min Serves - 4

INGREDIENTS

- 6 large potatoes (washed and peeled)
- 2 cloves of garlic or 1 tsp of garlic puree
- 1 tablespoon of butter
- 2 tablespoons of oil

METHOD

- Cut potatoes in to chunks or dice
- Bring to boil in saucepan of cold water and allow to simmer for 5 minutes
- Add oil to tray and heat in a hot oven
- Drain potatoes well and toss onto the tray
- Bake for 20 minutes turning half way through
- Melt butter and garlic in microwave and when fries are cooked add to tray and stir through until they are coated

Chicken & Vegetable Chow Mein

Prep - 10min Cook - 15min Serves - 4

INGREDIENTS

- 200g/7oz dried egg noodles (or rice or soba noodles)
- 1 large carrot
- 2 spring onions
- 50g/1¾oz peas (fresh or frozen)
- Baby sweetcorn, 2 peppers sliced, punnet of mushrooms, ½ a broccoli.
- 2 tsp vegetable or sunflower oil
- 1 garlic clove, finely chopped by an adult or crushed in a garlic press
- 2 cooked chicken breasts or 1 cup cooked prawns
- 2 tbsp soy sauce (low-salt version if possible)
- 3 tsp honey
- 2 tsp tomato ketchup
- 1 lemon juiced

METHOD

- Place the dried noodles in a heatproof bowl and add boiling water from the kettle. They will take approximately five minutes to cook. When the noodles are cooked, drain them in a sieve and rinse the noodles under cold water.
- Peel and grate the carrot, chop any other vegetables you want to include. Everything should be sliced thinly if possible.
- In a small bowl mix together the soy, honey, ketchup and lemon juice. Have a taste - it should be tangy but sweet. You can add a little more of the ingredients as needed.

Continued...

- Heat a large frying pan or wok and add the oil. Add the garlic and stir fry for a few seconds, then add the grated carrots, spring onions and the beans or peas (either raw or from frozen) as well as sliced cooked chicken or cooked prawns
- Stir fry for two minutes on a high heat before adding the sauce and a splash of water. Taste You may need extra honey, lemon or soy sauce.
- Add the cooked noodles to the stir-fried ingredients. Stir the chow mein for a couple of minutes over a high heat to finish the dish. Serve in a bowl - try using chopsticks!

Egg Fried Rice

Prep - 10min   Cook - 12min   Serves - 6

INGREDIENTS

- 1 tsp rapeseed oil
- 5 spring onions, thinly sliced
- 1 red pepper, seeds removed and thinly sliced
- 2 garlic cloves, finely chopped
- 1 head of broccoli, cut into small florets
- 1 tbsp soy sauce
- 300g/10½oz freshly cooked basmati rice, cooled
- 175g/6oz frozen peas
- 3 eggs, lightly beaten
- 2 tsp toasted sesame seeds
- sea salt and freshly ground black pepper

METHOD

- Heat a wok until hot, then add the oil. When it is hot, add the spring onions and red pepper and stir-fry for 1–2 minutes, or until just softened. Stir in the garlic and add the broccoli with 4 tablespoons of water, then bring to the boil and simmer for 2 minutes, or until the broccoli is just tender and the water has nearly evaporated.
- Add the rice and stir fry for 2–3 minutes, or until hot through. Stir in the peas and cook for 1 minute.
- Beat the eggs and soy sauce together using a fork. Add the egg mixture to the rice and stir-fry for 2–3 minutes, or until the eggs have just set. Stir in the sesame seeds, season with salt and pepper and serve immediately.

Roasted Chicken & Vegetable Tikka

Prep - 1 hr 15min Cook - 20min Serves - 4

INGREDIENTS

TIKKA

- 4 boneless chicken breasts
- 1 cup of plain greek yogurt
- 2 tablespoons of tikka curry powder
- 1 courgette
- 1 red pepper
- 1 green pepper
- 1 onion

MINT DIP

- 150g low fat Greek yogurt
- 1 tsp dried mint
- 1 tsp lemon juice
- 1 clove garlic
- (Mix all ingredients together)

METHOD

- Mix the yogurt and curry paste together in a bowl
- Cut chicken and vegetables into bite size pieces.
- Marinate for an hour at least.
- Shake off any excess marinade from chicken and vegetables, place in a large roasting tray and roast in a hot oven 180℃ for 15-20 minutes, turning once.
- When ready take out of tray, serve with warm pitta breads or tortillas with green salad and dip.

TIP: Make this in bulk and freeze in individual freezer bags and defrost when needed. Can be eaten cold for lunches or served with rice, cous cous or pasta

Creamy Healthy Slaw

Prep - 10min Serves - 4

INGREDIENTS

- 6 tbsp plain yogurt
- 2 tbsp mayonnaise
- 2 carrots
- ½ tsp sugar
- ½ tsp Dijon mustard
- ½ white cabbage
- ½ an onion
- Salt and black pepper

METHOD

- Mix the yogurt, mustard and mayonnaise together in a bowl.
- Slice cabbage thinly and grate carrots
- Chop or grate onion
- Tip all vegetables in a bowl and stir through the dressing
- This will keep in fridge for up to 3 days

No Yeast Naan Bread

Prep - 10min Cook - 15min Serves - 8

INGREDIENTS

- 260g self raising flour
- 1 tsp sugar
- 1 tsp baking powder
- Pinch of salt
- Cup of plain yogurt
- 2 tbsp of olive oil
- Splash of milk
- Melted butter
- Chopped coriander
- 2 cloves of garlic sliced thinly

METHOD

- Weigh out ingredients and put in a bowl
- Make a well in centre
- Add yogurt and mix.
- Add milk slowly to make a dough
- Knead for a couple of minutes
- Cut in half and roll out to oblong shape
- Add slices of garlic onto chopping board and roll into dough.
- Add chopped coriander and brush melted butter on top.
- Fry for 3 mins on each side in a hot pan.

Stuffed Baked Potato Boats

Prep - 20min Cook - 60min Serves - 2

INGREDIENTS

- 2 large potatoes
- 2 slices of ham
- 1 tomato
- 1 red pepper
- 2 tbsp of sweetcorn
- 1 knob of butter
- 2 oz of grated cheese

METHOD

- Scrub potatoes under running water
- Dry really well and pierce with a fork 2 or 3 times
- Wrap in Tinfoil and put into oven for 1 hr
- Take out and remove foil
- Cut in half lengthwise and remove the insides and put into a bowl
- Wash pepper and tomato and chop into dice
- Add these to the bowl with sweetcorn and chopped ham andbutter and season with salt and pepper
- Put back into the potatoes and sprinkle grated cheese on top
- Put back into oven until cheese is melted
- Serve with green veg such as broccoli or peas

Homemade Tomato and Vegetable Sauce

Prep - 10min Cook - 20min Serves - 6

The base of our tomato sauce contains Italian herbs, garlic, hidden vegetables including spinach, onions, mushrooms and is pureed. Kids love this too. Our recipe contains lots of nutrients and is a smooth pureed sauce.

This sauce is a game changer as it can be frozen in small tubs or bags and taken out when needed. We use it for some of the following recipes.

INGREDIENTS

- 1 large onion
- 1 red pepper
- 1 green pepper
- 1 yellow pepper
- 1 courgette
- 1 punnet of mushrooms
- 1 bag of Spinach or two blocks of frozen spinach.
- 3 tbs of tomato puree
- 2 tins of chopped tomatoes
- 1/2 pint of beef stock cube (1 beef stock cube)
- 2 cloves of garlic(crushed)
- 1 tsp oregano
- 1 tsp of basil (Or 2 tsp of Italian seasoning)
- olive oil for frying

METHOD

- Chop onion and fry gently in a medium saucepan
- Wash and chop peppers and mushrooms add to saucepan and add garlic, oregano basil and seasoning

Continued...

- Fry for 5 mins until vegetables are soft
- Add tomato puree and fry for 2 minutes, add tinned tomatoes or passata
- Add ½ tsp of sugar to take away bitter taste of tomatoes
- Make up the beef stock cube and add to pot
- Add washed spinach
- Bring to the boil and simmer for 10 mins

Meatballs & Wholemeal Spaghetti

Prep - 10min Cook - 20min Serves - 6

INGREDIENTS

- 2lb/ 1kg lean steak mince
- 1 onion (chopped finely)
- 1tbsp tomato puree
- 1 clove garlic (crushed)
- 3 cups of homemade tomato sauce
- ½ mug of dried breadcrumbs
- 1 large egg
- Salt and pepper to season
- 1 tsp oil

METHOD

- Heat up pan and add oil
- Add chopped onion and fry for 3 minutes until soft on a low/med heat
- Let onions cool down
- In a large bowl, add mince, puree, garlic, beaten egg, breadcrumbs and cooked onions
- Take a portion and roll it with clean hands into a ball, repeat with the rest of the mixture making sure they are all the same size
- Lay the meatballs out onto a tray that has been greased with small amount of oil. Roll the balls in the oil to coat
- Place in a hot oven to brown for 15 minutes

Continued...

- When meatballs are brown, transfer into a casserole dish
- Add Homemade tomato sauce and cover meatballs
- Cover with tin foil and bake at 180℃ gas mark 6 for 20 mins in hot oven
- Take out and add grated mozzarella cheese or grated cheddar to cover all meatballs and cook for 5 minutes or until cheese is bubbling
- Cook spaghetti according to the instructions on pack

Healthy Homemade Soda Bread Pizza

Prep - 30min Cook - 10min Serves - 4

This easy pizza recipe, provided by Neill's Flours is one of the favourites at our workshops. We make the dough using soda bread flour (if you don't have any you can use flour, baking powder, and bicarbonate soda). We also add butter milk and oil some seasoning and oregano to give an Italian flavour.

Children love playing with the dough, rolling it out, and shaping it into either pizza pie or rolled out flat on a pizza tray. Using toppings such as pineapple, peppers, cherry tomatoes and mushrooms means the children get to chop, cut, slice, taste and smell the ingredients and design their own making faces or shapes. Adding protein like chicken, ham or salami and pepperoni adds nutritional value too. The tomato sauce is our favourite recipe which is popular with the parents as it contains Italian herbs, garlic and hidden pureed vegetables. Kids love this too.

BASE

- 300g/10oz Soda Bread flour
- 250ml (approx) milk or buttermilk
- 4tbsp olive oil
- 2 tsp chopped herbs e.g. parsley, basil or ½ dried herbs

SAUCE

- Use 2 cups of Homemade Tomato sauce recipe for pizza.

TOPPINGS

- 1 block of Cheddar cheese
- 1 small bag of mozzarella cheese
- 1 bell pepper
- 2 tomatoes
- 1 pineapple
- 1 small pack of salami or pepperoni,
- 2 slices of ham,
- 1 punnet of mushrooms
- 1 small red onion

Continued...

To Make the Base

- Combine the sieved flour mix in a bowl with the herbs and olive oil. If using fresh herbs chop finely before adding
- Use the milk or buttermilk to mix to a soft dough
- Turn out onto a floured board, knead lightly then roll out to 1cm/½" thickness and approximately 20cm/8" diameter
- Place on a flat baking tray

To make up pizza

- Grate cheese
- Chop ham into bite size pieces
- Remove seeds from peppers and cut into dice
- Wash and dry mushrooms and chop into slices
- Take skin off pineapple, remove the stalk and chop into dice.
- Wash and dry mushrooms and chop into slices.
- Take skin off pineapple, remove the stalk and chop into dice.
- Wash, chop and dry tomatoes.

Continued...

- Add spoonfuls of pureed homemade tomato sauce onto pizza and add grated cheese and choice of meat, vegetables and fruit. Finish with grated cheese.
- Bake in oven at 200°C/Gas No 6 for 10- minutes or until well cooked.
- Remove from the oven, cut into wedges and serve either hot or cold on its own with salad.

CHAPTER

05

Weekend Chill out Recipes

Weekend Chill out Recipes

These dishes are family favourites in our house and they are great for getting everyone involved. We make the sauces, heat up tortillas wrapped in tinfoil in the oven, place all the sides in separate bowls and put onto the table so everyone can help themselves.

Get your children to make the salsa, mix the garlic dip and grate the cheese. They are really lovely family meals for a lazy Saturday or Sunday dinner!

Beef and Vegetable Tortillas

Prep - 20min Cook - 45min Serves - 8

INGREDIENTS

- 1 kg steak (5% fat) mince
- 1 large onion
- 1 red pepper
- 1 green pepper
- 1 yellow pepper
- 1 punnet of mushrooms
- Olive oil for frying
- 1 tin of kidney or mixed beans
- 2 cloves of garlic(crushed)
- 1 tsp mild chilli powder
- 1tsp cumin
- 1tsp paprika
- 2 tbsp of tomato puree
- 1 large carton of passata or 2 tins of chopped tomatoes
- ½ pint of beef stock cube made with 1 beef stock cube
- 8 wholemeal tortillas
- 6oz grated cheddar cheese

METHOD

Method for Meat Sauce

- Chop onion and fry gently in a medium saucepan
- Wash and chop peppers and mushrooms add to saucepan and add garlic, chilli, cumin and paprika. Fry with lid on for 5 mins until vegetables are soft
- Put mince in a frying pan until brown on a high heat
- Add tomato puree to pot of veg and add tinned tomatoes or passata
- Add ½ tsp of sugar to take away bitter taste of tomatoes
- Make up the beef stock cube and add to pot
- Add the browned mince to the sauce bring to the boil and simmer for about 20 minutes
- Meanwhile while sauce is cooking prepare the fillings

Continued...

INGREDIENTS

Guacamole

- 2 avocados - peeled, stones removed and chopped
- 1 small red onion, finely chopped
- 1 clove garlic, minced
- 1 ripe tomato, chopped
- 1 lime/lemon juiced
- salt and freshly ground black pepper to taste

Sour Cream Dip

- 150g low fat greek/plain yogurt
- 2 tbsp of low fat mayonnaise
- Juice of 1/2 lemon
- 1 crushed clove of garlic
- (Mix all ingredients together)

METHOD

For Tortillas

- Wrap tortillas in tinfoil and put into oven for 15 minutes at 150℃ gas mark 3
- When heated, place an individual tortilla on a plate, spread with sour cream, top with mince, cheese, salsa, and sour cream. Add grated cheese and roll up and enjoy
- Shredded iceberg lettuce and sliced red onion are delicious with this too.

For Guacamole

- Mash avocados in a medium serving bowl. Stir in onion, garlic, tomato and lime juice. Season with salt and pepper to taste.

Beef & Vegetable Stir Fry

Prep - 20min Cook - 15min Serves - 6

INGREDIENTS

- 1 cloves of garlic
- 1 fresh red chillies
- 1 large red pepper
- 1 small pack of baby corn
- 250g Fillet or sirloin steak
- Olive oil
- Light soy sauce
- 1oz sesame seeds
- 3 cm piece of ginger
- 3 spring onions
- 1 pack of mangetout/green beans
- Small bunch of fresh coriander
- 150 g dried medium free-range egg noodles (can get chilli ones for more flavour)
- Sesame oil

METHOD

- Toss the sesame seeds into clean pan and toast for 3-5 minutes until golden, put into a small dish.
- Cook the egg noodles in boiling salted water for 5 minutes according to the packet instructions, then drain and set aside.
- Peel and finely slice the garlic and ginger, trim and finely slice the chilli and spring onions, then deseed and finely slice the pepper.
- Cut Mangetout or green beans in half and quarter the baby corn lengthways
- Pick and roughly chop the coriander
- Using a separate chopping board thinly slice the steak.

Continued...

- Heat a tsp of olive oil in a large wok or a heavy-based frying pan over a high heat, add the beef slices, garlic, ginger and chillies and stir-fry until just cooked.
- Add a good splash of soy sauce and sesame oil and the lime juice for the last 30 seconds of cooking.
- Pour these ingredients into a large bowl and cover with a plate including all the juices.
- Put the wok back on the heat, drizzle in a splash more oil, then add all the vegetables. Stir-fry for 1 to 2 minutes, then add the cooked noodles and toss well over the heat.
- Divide the fried vegetables and noodles between 2 plates. Return the beef and juices to the wok and stir-fry until heated through.
- Add the coriander and toss until well mixed with the beef.
- Arrange on top of the noodles.
- Sprinkle the sesame seeds on top and serve.

Honey Chilli Chicken

Prep - 10min Cook - 15min Serves - 6

INGREDIENTS

- 3 tbsp soy sauce
- 2 tbsp honey
- Tomato ketchup
- 1 tbsp rice vinegar or white wine vinegar
- 1 tbsp brown sugar
- 2 tbsp sweet chilli sauce
- 100 ml water
- ¼ tsp garlic powder
- 4 chicken breasts
- 2 cloves of garlic crushed
- 2 large red or green peppers - cut into bite-sized pieces
- 2 tbsp cornflour
- ⅛ tsp (Pinch) of white pepper
- ¼ tsp salt
- Vegetable or sunflower oil
- 1 red chilli - de-seeded and chopped or ½ tsp chilli powder
- 2 onions

METHOD

- Mix the sauce ingredients together in a small jug or bowl and set aside.
- Mix the cornflour/ garlic powder, and optional white pepper in a medium-sized bowl that is large enough to hold the chicken pieces.
- Place the chicken pieces in the bowl and mix with your hands until they are evenly coated with the flour mixture.
- Put frying pan on a high heat and add around 0.5cm or ¼ inch oil. Add chicken when the oil is hot (Note 2) and fry for a couple of minutes on each side. Remove from the pan and set aside when it is crispy on the outside and cooked in the middle.

Continued...

- Carefully remove the excess oil from the pan or use a clean frying pan (you should be left with about a tablespoon - Note 4). Fry the chilli, garlic and ginger for 1-2 minutes until fragrant and add the peppers and fry for a few minutes until they begin to soften.
- Pour in the sauce let it reduce for a few seconds before adding the chicken pieces.
- Serve immediately with rice, topped with spring onions and toasted sesame seeds.

Cheesy Sweet Potato topped Cottage Pie

Prep - 45min Cook - 35min Serves - 6

INGREDIENTS

- 1 tablespoon olive oil
- 1 large onion, finely chopped
- 1 large carrot, peeled, finely chopped
- 2 celery stalks, trimmed, finely chopped
- 500g beef mince
- 2 tsps Worcestershire sauce
- 2 tbsp tomato puree
- 1 tin 400g of chopped tomatoes
- 1 teaspoon mixed herbs
- 1 cup of frozen peas
- 2 large sweet potatoes peeled, chopped
- 6 large potatoes peeled and chopped
- 1 beef stock cube dissolved in ¼ cup of boiling water
- 1/4 cup milk
- 20g butter
- 1/2 cup grated cheddar cheese

METHOD

- Heat oil in large saucepan over medium heat. Add onion, carrot and celery.
- Cook, stirring, for 3 to 4 minutes or until onion has softened.
- Add mince. Cook, stirring with a wooden spoon to break up mince, for 5 minutes or until browned.
- Add tomato puree and fry for 2-3 minutes
- Add Worcestershire sauce, tinned tomato and herbs.
- Bring to the boil. Reduce heat to low. Simmer for 20 to 25 minutes or until thickened. Stir in peas. Preheat oven to 180°C

Continue...

- Meanwhile, cook both potatoes together in a saucepan of boiling water for 8 minutes or until just tender.
- Drain then return to pan. Add milk and butter. Mash until smooth.
- Spoon beef mixture into a medium sized deep oven dish.
- Top with potato mixture and sprinkle with cheese.
- Bake for 30 to 35 minutes or until golden.
- Serve.

Chicken Korma

Prep - 20min Cook - 25min Serves - 6

INGREDIENTS

- 4 X breasts chicken
- 2 tsp sunflower oil
- 40 g butter
- 2 onions
- 3 tsp ginger
- 2 cloves garlic
- 2 tsp ground cumin
- 2 tbsp toasted flaked almonds
- Fresh coriander leaves
- 1 tin light coconut milk
- 2 tsp ground coriander
- 6-8 crushed cardamom pods
- Ground cloves
- Pinch of cinnamon
- 1 tsp turmeric
- ½ tsp mild chilli powder/or 1 fresh chilli
- 2 tbsp mango chutney or 3 tsp caster sugar
- 1 mug of chicken stock (1 stock cube)
- Serve with rice

METHOD

- Cut each chicken breast into small chunks (roughly 2.5cm) and season generously with freshly ground black pepper.
- Heat oil in a large non-stick frying pan or wok and fry the chicken over a medium-high heat for 5-6 mins, turning occasionally.
- Transfer the chicken to a plate using a slotted spoon or spatula and return the pan to the heat. Keep the chicken warm by covering in foil or placing in the oven on a low heat.

Continued...

- Add the remaining oil, butter and onions to the pan and cook over a medium heat, stirring often, for 10 mins, or until the onions are soft and lightly browned. Stir in the ginger and garlic paste and ground spices and cook, stirring continuously, for a further 1 min.
- Add the mango chutney and stock to the spiced onions and bring to a simmer. Cook for 5 mins or until the liquid has reduced by roughly half, stirring regularly. (For an extra smooth sauce, blitz the mixture with a blender.)
- Return the chicken to the pan with the onions, add the coconut milk and simmer gently, stirring occasionally, for 5-6 mins, until the chicken is piping hot and cooked through. Add a splash of water to loosen the sauce if necessary.
- Garnish the curry with toasted flaked almonds and scatter with fresh coriander, if you like. Serve with our perfect rice recipe (below).
- This delicious creamy curry can also be served with our naan bread recipe from earlier in the book!

Perfect Rice

Cook - 10min Serves - 4

INGREDIENTS

- 2 mugs of brown rice
- 4 mugs of boiling water

METHOD

- Measure out rice into pot, add boiling water, stir once and bring back to the boil
- Allow to simmer for 10 minutes with the lid on

Homemade Beef and Vegetable Burgers

Prep - 15min Cook - 15min Serves - 8

BURGER INGREDIENTS

- 450 g low fat mince meat
- 1 medium onion
- 1 red pepper
- 1 green pepper
- 1 tsp veg oil
- Grated cheese
- 1 tsp dried mixed herbs
- 1 chicken stock cube
- 25 g breadcrumbs
- 1 granny smith apple (peeled and grated)
- 1 egg

SAUCE INGREDIENTS

- 5 tbsp of low fat mayonnaise
- 3 tbsp of tomato ketchup
- 1 tbsp of chopped pickles
- 1 tsp English mustard

METHOD

- Preheat oven to 180℃ or gas mark 6
- Put mince into a large bowl and season
- Chop onion and pepper into small dice and fry in oil for 5 minutes until soft
- Let it cool and then add to meat
- Add herbs, stock cube and breadcrumbs
- Grate apple and add this along with egg with clean hands
- Shape into burgers
- Place onto an oven tray and cook for 15 minutes, turning once
- Serve with wheaten baps, salad and cheese and burger sauce

Sweet Potato Fries

Prep - 5min   Cook - 30min   Serves - 6

FRIES INGREDIENTS

- 8 sweet potatoes
- 2 tbsp Olive oil
- Garlic
- Smoked paprika

SWEET CHILLI DIP

- 1 tbsp of sweet chilli sauce
- 3 tbsp of low-fat mayonnaise
- (Mix all ingredients together)

METHOD

- Wash potatoes, cut into chips and put into large bowl
- Add garlic and paprika and oil
- Mix until all chips are covered and place onto hot roasting tray
- Roast in hot oven 190°C gas mark 6-7 for 30 mins turning once

Chicken and Vegetable Fajitas

Prep - 15min   Cook - 20min   Serves - 4

INGREDIENTS

- 1 x pack 8 whole meal flour tortillas
- 4 chicken breasts, cut into strips
- 2 cloves of garlic or 2 tsp garlic powder
- 1 tsp ground cumin
- 1 ½ tsp mild chilli powder
- Lemon juice
- 4 tomatoes (washed and sliced)
- Homemade garlic mayonnaise
- Salsa
- 1 bag grated cheese
- 3 tbsp olive oil
- 2 onion, thinly sliced
- 3 peppers, preferably different colours, thinly sliced
- 1 punnet of mushrooms (washed, dried and chopped)
- Salt and freshly ground black pepper
- 1 Iceberg lettuce (washed and chopped)

METHOD

- Heat the oven to 120°C/100°C Fan/Gas ½. Wrap the tortillas in kitchen foil, place on a baking tray and warm in the oven until ready to use.
- Put the chicken in a bowl with the garlic, cumin, chilli powder and lemon juice. Season with salt and pepper and toss, rubbing the seasoning into the chicken. Set aside to marinade for 5 minutes.
- Heat 1 tablespoon of the oil in a frying pan over a high heat. Add the chicken strips and cook for 5 minutes, until cooked through, golden-brown and slightly catching on the edges.
- Add the remaining 1 tablespoon of oil to the pan, add the onion, mushroom and peppers and fry for 5 minutes, or until almost soft.

To assemble the fajitas

- Spread the garlic mayonnaise on top the warmed tortillas with the chicken and vegetable mix
- Add salsa and top with lettuce, tomatoes and grated cheese
- Roll up and enjoy!

CHAPTER

06

Vegetarian Favourites

Homemade Falafels

Prep - 15min Cook - 60min Serves - 6

INGREDIENTS

- 2 tbsp olive oil
- 1 small onion, finely chopped
- 1 garlic clove, crushed
- 1 x 400g/14oz can chickpeas
- 2 tsp ground cumin
- Salt and black pepper
- Pinch of chilli flakes
- ½ tsp tahini(opt)
- 1/2 tsp of caraway seeds
- 1 tsp mixed herbs
- 1 lemon, zest grated
- 1 egg, beaten

TO SERVE

- Wholemeal pitta bread
- Leaves from 1 little gem lettuce (90g)
- Herb Dip
- 2 large tomatoes (160g), sliced
- 1 large red onion (80g), thinly sliced.

METHOD

- Heat a tablespoon of oil in a small pan. Fry the onion over a medium heat for 3-4 minutes until softened.
- Add the garlic and fry for a further two minutes and remove from the heat.
- Drain and rinse the chickpeas and transfer to a mixing bowl.
- Add the sautéed onion and garlic and crush together with a potato masher until the mixture is broken down.
- Add the cumin, mixed herbs and lemon zest and mix well. Taste and season with salt and pepper.

Continued...

- Add the egg and mix together.
- Preheat the oven to 200°C/400°F/Gas 6. Divide the mixture into 16 walnut-sized balls and place on a non-stick baking tray. Rest in the fridge for 20-30 minutes.
- Remove the falafel from the fridge, drizzle with the remaining oil and bake for 25 minutes, or until crisp and golden-brown. Turn occasionally to ensure even cooking.
- Meanwhile place the cucumber, tomato and lettuce in a large bowl. Squeeze the juice of half the lemon into a small bowl, add a pinch of salt and pepper and using a fork whisk together with the olive oil to form a dressing. Pour over the salad and mix well.
- Lightly toast the pitta breads then carefully slice open along one side using a knife.
- When ready to serve, arrange a little salad in each pitta, top with some of the falafels and add a squeeze of juice from the remaining lemon half. Serve with the remaining salad and herb dip.

Greek Salad

Prep - 10min Serves - 6

INGREDIENTS

DRESSING

- ¼ cup extra-virgin olive oil
- 3 tablespoons red or white wine vinegar
- 1 garlic clove, minced
- ½ teaspoon dried oregano, more for sprinkling
- ¼ teaspoon Dijon mustard
- ¼ teaspoon sea salt
- Freshly ground black pepper

SALAD

- 1 cucumber, cut lengthwise, seeded, and sliced ¼-inch thick
- 1 green bell pepper, chopped into 1-inch pieces
- 1 punnet of halved cherry tomatoes
- 5 ounces feta cheese , cut into ½ inch cubes*
- ½ sliced red onion
- ⅓ cup pitted olives
- fresh mint leaves

METHOD

- Make the dressing: In a small bowl, whisk together the olive oil, vinegar, garlic, oregano, mustard, salt, and several grinds of pepper.
- On a large platter, arrange the cucumber, green pepper, cherry tomatoes, feta cheese, red onions, and olives.
- Drizzle with the dressing and very gently toss. Sprinkle with a few generous pinches of oregano and top with the mint leaves. Season to taste and serve.

Sweet Potato Wedges

Prep - 10min Cook - 30min Serves - 4

WEDGES INGREDIENTS

- 8 sweet potatoes
- 2 tbsp olive oil
- Garlic
- Smoked paprika

HERB DIP INGREDIENTS

- 1 tbsp of crème fraiche
- 1 tbsp of low fat Greek yogurt
- 1 tsp of dried parsley
- 1 tsp of dried tarragon
- Salt and pepper
- Juice of half a lemon
- (Mix all together)

METHOD

- Preheat the oven to 190C/ Gas 6-7 and preheat roasting tray
- Wash potatoes, cut into wedges, put into large freezer bag
- Add garlic, paprika and oil
- Shake until all wedges are covered
- Place onto hot roasting tray and cook for 30 minutes turning once

Curry Flavoured Rice & Vegetables

Prep - 8min Cook - 15min Serves - 6

INGREDIENTS

- 1 Onion
- 2 tbsp curry powder
- ½ tsp ground chilli
- 2 mugs brown rice
- 1 red pepper
- 1 Clove garlic(crushed)
- ½ tsp ground ginger
- 4 mugs of boiling water

METHOD

- Chop and dice all vegetables
- Heat olive oil in pan and add vegetables
- Add spices and garlic and fry over a low heat until soft.
- Add rice, stir well and add boiling water, bring to boil and stir .
- Allow to simmer for 10 minutes on a gentle heat, be careful not to burn bottom of the pan.
- Can be served cold, as a salad, for lunches. Add extra or different veg if required.

Slow Cooker Vegetable Chili

Prep - 20min Serves - 6

Slow Cook - 3hr (high)/5-6hrs (low) Hob - 45min

INGREDIENTS

- 2 teaspoons sunflower oil
- ½ butternut squash diced
- 1 onion, chopped
- 1 green or red pepper, seeded and diced
- 2 cloves garlic, crushed
- 1 Courgette chopped
- 2 blocks of frozen spinach
- 1 large fresh green chilli, seeded and finely chopped
- 2 teaspoons ground cumin
- 1 teaspoon mild chilli powder
- 400g (14oz) can chopped tomatoes
- Smoked paprika
- 1 tin sweet corn
- 1 tablespoon tomato purée
- 2 carrots, diced
- 250ml (9fl oz) vegetable stock
- Freshly ground black pepper, to taste
- 420g (15oz) can red kidney beans, rinsed and drained
- 420g can of Mixed beans
- Chopped fresh coriander, to garnish

METHOD

- Preheat oven to 180°C/350°F/Gas Mark 4 or turn on slow cooker to high. Heat oil in pot on hob
- Add onion, sweet potato, carrot, courgette, pepper, garlic and chilli and sauté for 10 minutes or until softened
- Add cumin and chilli powder, smoked paprika and cook gently for 1 minute, stirring. Stir in tomatoes, tomato purée, celery, stock and black pepper
- Add drained tinned beans and sweetcorn
- Bring to boil, pour into slow cooker and cook on high for 3 hours or on low for 5-6 hours
- Garnish with chopped coriander and serve with boiled brown or rice or Plain baked potatoes

Spicy Bean Burgers

Prep - 10min Cook - 10min Serves - 6

BURGER INGREDIENTS

- 1 slice wholemeal bread, crumbled
- 1 egg, beaten
- 400g tin mixed beans, drained and rinsed (240g)
- 2 tsp mild smoked paprika
- 1 tsp oregano
- Pinch chilli flakes
- 2 cloves garlic, crushed
- 2 onions (160g), grated
- 1 large carrot (160g), grated.

SAUCE INGREDIENTS

- 5 tbsp of low fat mayonnaise
- 3 tbsp of tomato ketchup
- 1 tbsp of chopped pickles
- 1 tsp English mustard

TO SERVE

- Wholemeal bap
- Leaves from 1 little gem lettuce (90g)
- 2 large tomatoes (160g), sliced
- 1 large red onion (80g), thinly sliced.

METHOD

- In a bowl, with a fork mix the bread with the egg to create a rough paste
- Place the beans in a large bowl and roughly mash. Stir in the remaining ingredients and combine well, then add the bread and egg mixture and mix together (with your hands is best) until everything is combined
- Divide the mixture into 4 and form each into patties or burgers
- Place on a nonstick baking sheet and grill for 4–5 minutes each side
- Serve in a wholemeal roll filled with lettuce, tomatoes, red onion and sauce.

Pasta & Cheese With Vegetables

Prep - 20min   Cook - 25-30min   Serves - 6

INGREDIENTS

- 1 pinch salt
- 500g 1 bag pasta (penne)
- 1 drop vegetable oil
- 1 ½ oz of butter
- 1 ½ oz of plain flour
- 1 ½ pint semi skimmed milk
- 1 ½ tsp mustard
- 3 oz cheddar cheese (grated)
- 1 or veg stock cube dissolved in a little hot water.
- 2 carrots (washed peeled and grated)
- 1 head broccoli (washed and cut into small florets)
- Handful of Frozen Peas
- 6 oz Bread crumbs
- 2 oz grated cheese
- 4 tomatoes, sliced

METHOD

- Melt the butter in a heavy based saucepan
- Add flour, stir well and cook on a gentle heat for 2 mins to cook out the flour
- Remove from the heat and slowly add milk using a whisk
- Bring back to the boil over a medium heat
- Add cheese and mustard and stock, season well
- Cook pasta according to pack and drain
- Prepare vegetables and put into large oven dish
- Add pasta to oven dish
- Cover with cheese sauce
- Sprinkle breadcrumbs and grated cheese over and decorate with tomatoes
- Bake for 25-30 minutes at 180℃ gas mark 6
- Serve with garlic bread (next page)

Homemade Garlic Bread

Prep - 10min Cook - 15min Serves - 6

INGREDIENTS

- 2 medium wholemeal crusty baguettes
- Fresh parsley (chopped)
- Salt and pepper
- 2 cloves of garlic
- 4 oz butter
- Juice of half a lemon

METHOD

- Add butter, crushed garlic, salt and lemon juice into a medium sized bowl and mix well
- Using a serrated edged knife slice diagonally in slices but not all the way through the bread. Open each slice and spread butter in between each slice.
- Wrap the baguettes in tinfoil and bake in a hot oven 180℃ for 10 minutes and then open up the foil and continue cooking for 5 minutes.
- Remove from the oven and slice and serve with cannelloni.
- Serve with green mixed leaves salad

CHAPTER

07

Fish Favourites

Fish Favourites

One of the most important nutrients found in oil-rich fish is omega-3 fats. These special fats cannot be made in the body so it is important that we get them from the food we eat. Omega-3 fats are particularly important for children as they play an essential role in the early development of the brain and nerves. Almost 60% of the brain is made up of fat and half of this is omega 3 fats. While in the womb the baby gets omega-3 fats from the foods the mother eats, but after birth they need to get them from breast or fortified formula milk. As they move away from breast or formula milk, children need to start getting more omega-3 fats from their food to allow the brain to continue to develop and grow.

There is a great deal of research into the potential role of omega-3 fats in protecting memory and in preventing and treating conditions like dyslexia and ADHD (Attention Deficit Hyperactivity Disorder).

Diseases like heart disease are becoming more common and omega-3 fats help to protect against heart disease. Getting children into a good habit of eating fish will help not only to encourage healthy growth and development but also to help protect against some of the diseases of adult life (11).

It's recommended that children eat two portions of fish a week, one of which should be oily fish, for example, salmon, sardines, mackerel or trout. It's recommended that boys have no more than four portions of oily fish a week, and girls no more than two portions a week because oily fish can contain low level of pollutants that can build up in the body.

The health benefits of eating oily fish are greater than the risks, so do try and encourage children to eat fish regularly.

Salmon, Kale and Potato Fish cakes with Salsa

Prep - 30min   Cook - 1hr 15min   Serves - 6

INGREDIENTS

- 500g potatoes chopped into dice
- 2 darnes of salmon (270 g pk)
- I/2 bag kale/cabbage
- 3 scallions/1 onion
- 1tbs of butter
- Seasoning
- ¼ tsp English mustard
- 1/4 tsp Dill
- 1 clove of crushed garlic
- 1 egg
- 1 tsp olive oil

METHOD

- Preheat oven to 180°c
- Peel and wash potatoes add cold water and bring to boil and simmer till ready
- Meanwhile sprinkle dill and lemon on salmon and put in tin foil in oven dish, add a splash of water to dish
- Bake for 15 mins at 180°C for 20 mins
- Wash kale and leave to steep with salt to remove any dirt
- Chop scallions/onion and melt with butter until soft (in microwave for 2 mins)
- Steam or boil kale until soft. Drain well and squeeze liquid out using a plate
- When potatoes are cooked add salt, pepper, 1 tsp English mustard and melted butter and scallions

Continued...

- Add kale ensuring it is not too wet
- Remove skin from salmon and flake fish into the mash potatoes
- Add dill and garlic and season well
- Add egg to mash and mix well
- Shape mix into round patties/ cakes with your hands
- Sprinkle with sesame seeds and set on tray and chill for 30 mins to set

TO COOK

- Heat a tray with the olive oil and when hot place salmon cakes on to it and bake in oven for 15 mins
- Or fry in tsp of olive oil on pan on med heat for 15 mins turning once

TO SERVE

- Serve with salsa and roasted vegetables

Salmon Bites

Cook - 15min   Serves - 4

INGREDIENTS

- 300g skinless boneless salmon fillets, cut into dice
- 2tbsp plain flour
- 1 egg, beaten
- 75g breadcrumbs
- 20g sesame seeds
- Zest of 2 lemons
- Sunflower oil for shallow frying
- Lemon wedges, to serve
- 1 tbsp basalmic vinegar

METHOD

- Put the fish pieces into a large bowl and add the plain flour.
- Season well and toss altogether until the fish pieces are well coated.
- In a separate bowl, mix together the breadcrumbs and lemon zest and sesame seeds.
- Dip each piece in the beaten egg, then in the breadcrumbs to coat.
- Heat a baking tray with 2 tbsp olive oil in oven
- Put fish onto tray and coat each one with oil.
- Bake in hot oven 180°C for 15 minutes until golden brown and cooked through.
- Drizzle with balsamic vinegar
- Serve with champ (next page)

Champ

Prep - 15min   Cook - 20min

INGREDIENTS

- 100g spring onion, cut into rings
- 100ml full-fat milk
- 900g mashing potato, such as King Edward or Maris Piper
- 85-100g/3-4oz butter
- 50 ml fresh cream
- extra butter, for serving
- Fresh parsley

METHOD

- Peel and wash the potatoes then quarter them. Cover with cold water and bring to the boil, simmer for 12-15 minutes until soft.
- Drain the water from them, remove from the heat and cover with lid half on them to allow them to continue steaming.
- Put the spring onions and milk in a small pan and heat to boiling. Take off the heat and leave to infuse.
- Remove from the heat and mash the potatoes with the butter until no lumps are left. Add the milk and the spring onions, then gradually beat this into the potatoes, mixing well with a wooden spoon to make the potatoes fluffy.
- Add fresh cream, season well.

Homemade Fish Fingers

Prep - 10min Cook - 15min Serves - 4

INGREDIENTS

- 300g white fish, skinless boneless fillets, cut into thick strips
- 2tbsp plain flour
- 1 egg, beaten
- 75g breadcrumbs
- Sesame/pumpkin seeds
- Zest of 2 lemons
- Sunflower oil for shallow frying
- Lemon wedges, to serve

METHOD

- Put the fish pieces into a large bowl and add the plain flour.
- Season well and toss altogether until the fish pieces are well coated.
- In a separate bowl, mix together the breadcrumbs and lemon zest.
- Dip each piece in the beaten egg, then in the breadcrumbs to coat.
- Heat a baking tray with 2 tbsp olive oil in oven
- Put fish onto tray and coat each one with oil.
- Bake in hot oven 180°C for 15 minutes until golden brown and cooked through.
- Serve with Herb Dip from page 83

Salmon and Spinach Pasta Bake

Prep - 15min   Cook - 25min   Serves - 6

INGREDIENTS

- Four salmon darnes or 1lb of salmon whole (deboned)
- I bag wholewheat pasta (white if prefered)
- 1 bg fresh spinach(washed)or 3 blocks of frozen spinach
- 1 punnet of cherry tomatoes
- 1 punnet mushrooms
- 1 onion
- 3Tbsp of pesto
- 1/2tsp dill
- 1 tub low fat Cream cheese
- Juice of 1 lemon
- Olive oil 1 tsp

METHOD

- Put salmon, cherry tomatoes, dill, lemon juice in oven dish, cover with foil and bake in oven 180℃ for 20 mins
- Meanwhile cook pasta according to instructions
- Chop onion and mushroom and fry gentle in med size pot until soft, add spinach put lid in and steam for 5 mins, stirring in between
- When pasta is cooked pour into deep oven dish, add salmon and tomatoes, add vegetables and mix in cream cheese and pesto, smooth out and add grated cheese
- Put back in oven for a couple of minutes and brown
- Serve with salad

CHAPTER 08

Baking

Baking

I got my love of cooking from baking when I was very young and I think this is really important skill to have. My Granny taught me to bake in her wee scullery on Sunday mornings. I loved to help her as she made fruit cakes, egg sponges and apple tarts.

My granny (left) and her bowl (right) which I'm delighted to still have and use to this day. It is likely over 50 years old!

My Mum always encouraged me to cook and bake and as the oldest girl she was probably glad of the break! My Dad gave me the Ballymaloe cookbook when I was 10 and I was hooked. They had delicious recipes for scones, bread and cakes so I used this a lot and I still have it.

At Wyse Bites we encourage parents to try bread making and often the children with food aversions will use the bread as a bridge to try the new foods such as hummus, dips, and soups. Our recipe for wholegrain bread with sesame seeds is a must try. We also have a recipe for soda bread that is easy to make.

Soda Bread

Prep - 10min Cook - 30min Makes - 1 Loaf

INGREDIENTS

- 1lb of flour, self raising
- 1 tsp salt
- ½ tsp bicarbonate of soda
- 14 fl oz buttermilk

METHOD

- Put dry ingredients into a large bowl, sieve the bic of soda to remove lumps.
- Add the buttermilk slowly and using hand mix into a sticky dough
- Do not knead, dust with flour and flip it over into a ball and flatten gently with hand.
- Mark with a cross, pinch each quarter
- Bake for 15-20 minutes @ 220°C gas mark 7 for 15 minutes and then turn down oven to 200°C gas mark 6 for a further 15 minutes.
- When you knock the bottom of the bread and it sounds hollow then it is ready.
- Wrap in a tea towel to cool.

Healthy Banana Bread

Prep - 10min Cook - 35min Makes - 1 1lb Loaf

INGREDIENTS

DRY

- 4oz mug wholemeal (med) flour
- 4 oz mug plain flour
- 1/2 tsp baking powder
- 1 tsp baking soda
- 1/2 tsp salt
- 3 oz castor sugar

WET

- 1 egg
- 1/8 cup of oil
- 1/2 cup of yogurt
- 1 tsp vanilla extract
- 3 bananas

METHOD

- Preheat oven to 180°C
- Put all dry ingredients into a mixing bowl
- Mix wet ingredients together in a separate mixing bowl
- Add the wet ingredients to dry ingredients and combine
- Pour into 1lb loaf tin and bake for about 35 mins or until a knife comes out clean
- Note: If you have a food mixer the ingredients can be all added and mixed together. If not, mix separately and combine as outlined above.

Brown Bread with Treacle and Sesame Seeds

Prep - 10min Cook - 30min Makes - 2 Loaves

This is an easy recipe as it contains one bowl for wet and one for dry, then mix, great for getting children to eat more fibre and can be used to dip in the soups.

INGREDIENTS

DRY

- 400g coarse wholemeal flour
- 100g plain flour
- 50 g sesame seeds or a mix of seeds
- 1 tsp baking soda
- 1 tsp salt
- 1 tbsp sesame seeds for sprinkling

WET

- 1 tsp treacle
- 400ml buttermilk
- 1 egg
- 2 tbsp sunflower oil

METHOD

- Preheat oven to 200°C. Oil the loaf tin
- Place the dry ingredients in baking bowl and mix thoroughly. Make a well in the centre
- Place the treacle in a measuring jug, add the buttermilk and stir to mix. Add the beaten egg and oil
- Pour the wet ingredients into the dry ingredients and mix with a wooden spoon to form soft and sloppy dough
- Pour the dough into the prepared tins and draw a line lengthways through the top of the loaf before sprinkling with the sesame seeds
- Bake for approximately 30 mins

Scones

Prep - 10min Cook - 15min Makes - 8

This recipe is one that I use quite regularly, the scones are crunchy on the outside and soft inside. Served with whipped cream, strawberry jam and dusted with icing sugar they are a great way to get children interested in baking. Adding sultanas, apples, raspberries or cherries also adds to the national value of them. To increase the fibre content, add 50g of wholemeal medium flour. They require very little handling, when the dough is made tip onto a floured surface, gently shape into a ball and flatten it but not too thin. A favourite in our house at the weekends and they can be frozen and heated in the oven for about 8 minutes at 180°C

INGREDIENTS

- 1 tsp baking powder
- 1 oz sugar
- 1 egg
- Choose from 1 tsp of Cinnamon, Ginger, Nutmeg, All spice Chocolate for drizzling.
- 8oz flour (2 oz wholemeal flour and 6oz self raising flour)
- 2 oz butter (cold cut into cubes)
- About 110ml (3 fl oz) milk
- 2 oz fruit, (apple, pear, blueberries, strawberries, sultanas)

METHOD

- Preheat the oven to 200°C (fan 190°C/425°F/Gas 6). Lightly flour a large baking sheet.
- Put the flour and baking powder into a large mixing bowl. Add the cubes of butter, keeping all the ingredients as cold as possible.

Continued...

- Rub in lightly and quickly with your fingertips until the mixture looks like fine breadcrumbs. Add the sugar and choice of fruit and flavouring.
- Pour 50 ml of the milk and all but 1 tablespoons of the beaten egg into the flour mixture. Mix together with a round-bladed knife to a soft, but not too sticky dough, adding a bit more milk if needed to mop up any dry bits of mixture in the bottom of the bowl.
- Turn the dough out onto a lightly floured work surface, lightly knead just a few times only until gathered together, then gently roll and pat out to form a rectangle about 2cm (¾in) deep.
- Cut out as many rounds as possible from the first rolling with a 6cm (2½in) cutter (a plain cutter is easier to use than a fluted one) and lay them on the baking sheet, spaced slightly apart.
- Gather the trimmings, then roll and cut out again. Repeat until you have 6 scones.
- Brush the tops of the scones with the reserved egg. Bake for about 10 minutes, or until risen and golden.
- Remove and cool on a wire rack.
- Melt chocolate and drizzle over cooled scones
- Serve with cream and jam.

Carrot Cake

Prep - 10min Cook - 30min Makes - 1 Loaf

A good source of protein and vitamin A Serves 6

CAKE INGREDIENTS

- 155 ml sunflower oil and some for greasing
- 230g self-raising flour
- 1 tsp baking powder
- 1 ½ tsp ground cinnamon
- ½ tsp mixed spice
- ½ tsp ground ginger
- 230g light brown muscovado sugar
- Finely grated zest of 1 satsuma or mandarin
- 260 g carrots grated coarsely
- 3 medium eggs beaten

ICING INGREDIENTS

- 50 g butter softened
- 200g full-fat cream cheese
- 100g icing sugar plus extra to dust
- Finely grated zest of 1 orange

METHOD

- Preheat the oven to 180°C/fan 160°C /gas mark 4
- Grease an 18cm loose bottom tin and line the base with baking paper.
- Sift the flour, baking powder and spices into a large bowl.
- Add the sugar, zest, and grated carrots then stir until well combined.

Continued...

- Stir in the beaten eggs and oil and mix well.
- Pour into the prepared cake tin and bake in the oven for 1 hr or until skewer comes out clean.
- Transfer to a cooling rack, leave in the tin for 5 minutes then turn out to cool completely before icing.
- Beat the butter in a large bowl with a hand mixer until really soft.
- Add the cream cheese and beat again until well mixed
- Sift over the icing sugar, add the orange zest then beat until smooth
- When cake is cooled spread over the top and serve.

Homemade Buns

Prep - 15min   Cook - 15min   Makes - 12

We use this recipe for our children's baking workshops and cupcake birthday parties. It is a favourite and it never fails.

INGREDIENTS

- 8oz butter
- 8oz self raising flour
- 3 eggs
- 8oz castor sugar
- 1 tsp baking powder

METHOD

- Cream butter and sugar together
- Beat eggs together
- Sieve flour and baking powder
- Add half ofeggs to sugar and butter mix
- Then add half of flour
- Repeat this
- Add a drop of milk at the end and drop of vanilla essence
- Put into lined muffin trays
- Bake in oven 180°C or gas mark 6 for 15-20 minutes
- Remove from tins and allow to cool on a wire tray

Chocolate Chip Cookies

Prep - 10min   Cook - 8-10min   Makes - 12

INGREDIENTS

- 115 g / 4 oz margarine
- 2 tbsp milk
- Vanilla extract
- 170 /6 oz self raising flour
- 85g / 3 oz light brown sugar
- 2 tbsp golden syrup
- 112 g /4 oz choc chips

METHOD

- Preheat oven
- 180°C or gas mark 4
- Cream margarine and sugar
- Add the milk, golden syrup, vanilla and s r flour
- Add chocolate chips to the mix to make a smooth batter
- Place spoonfuls onto a greased and floured tray or grease proof paper, spaced out.
- Bake for 8- 10 minutes allow to cool and put onto a rack.
- Decorate with icing/ melted chocolate and sprinkles.

Apple Tart

My Dad always got me to bake him an apple tart on Sundays so myself and my friend Teresa took turns baking in each other's houses. We always ended up making 2 or 3 as 1 was never enough. I loved to make the dough following my Grannies recipe and peeling the apples always turned into a competition to see whose peel could stay on the peeler the longest. Then of course we dipped the skins into sugar while it was baking and left a mess for our poor Mum's to clean up.

This recipe will make 1 dinner plate size apple tart and the pastry can be made in advance and frozen. Children love to play with this dough as it is nice and soft. It can also be used to make jam tarts too.

Apple Tart

Prep - 20min (+ 1hr in fridge) Cook - 30-35min Serves - 6

INGREDIENTS

- 8oz plain flour
- 3oz sugar
- 1 egg
- 2 large cooking apples
- 4oz butter
- Drop of milk if it's too dry
- 3tbsp sugar for apples

METHOD

- Add butter to flour and make it like breadcrumbs
- Add the sugar
- Mix beaten egg and enough milk to form a soft dough
- Put it in fridge for at least an hour.
- Peel and chop 2-3 Bramley apples
- Add lemon juice to stop them going brown
- Add sugar
- When pastry is chilled
- Cut in 2 and roll out and put onto a greased plate.
- Add apples
- Roll out remainder of dough and put on top.
- Press with a fork around the sides to make a crust.
- Brush with egg and bake in oven 180℃ gas mark 6 for 30 -35 minutes or until golden brown.

Apple Crumble

Prep - 20min   Cook - 40min   Serves - 6

My sons would often make this during the winter for Sunday dessert when we get lots of apples from our cousin. Its really easy to make and is delicious with custard. You can also add frozen or fresh berries to it to bulk it up. The kitchen was always a mess so I suppose it was payback for the mess I left our kitchen in when I was younger! My Austrian friend Katrin says this is the best apple crumble in Europe !

INGREDIENTS

- 3 large apples - peeled, cored, and sliced
- 90g brown sugar
- 60g oats
- 120 g plain flour
- 2 tablespoons caster sugar
- 1 teaspoon ground cinnamon
- 120g cold butter

METHOD

- Preheat oven to 180℃ / Gas 4.
- Toss apples with 2tbsps caster sugar and 1/2 teaspoon cinnamon in a medium bowl to coat; pour into a baking dish.
- Mix brown sugar, oats, flour and 1 teaspoon cinnamon in a separate bowl. Mash cold butter into the oats mixture until the mixture resembles coarse crumbs; spread over the apples to the edges of the baking dish. Pat the topping gently until even.
- Bake in preheated oven until golden brown and sides are bubbling, about 40 minutes.

Rocky Road Traybakes

Prep - 15min Cook - 2hrs Serves - 6

INGREDIENTS

- 200g (8 oz) digestive biscuits
- 135g (5 ½ oz) butter or margarine
- 200g (8 oz) milk chocolate
- 2-3 tbsp golden syrup
- 100 g (4 oz) mini marshmallows
- 50g (2oz)Maltesers
- Melted white chocolate buttons and sprinkles for the top

METHOD

- Grease and line an 18cm square brownie tin with baking paper.
- Place 200g digestive biscuits in a freezer bag and bash with a rolling pin or just the side of your fist until they're broken into a mixture of everything between dust and 50p-sized lumps. Set aside.
- In a large saucepan, melt 135g butter or margarine, 200g dark chocolate and 2-3 tbsp golden syrup over a gentle heat stirring constantly until there are little or no lumps of chocolate visible, then remove from the heat. Leave to cool.
- Take the biscuits, 100g mini marshmallows and Maltesers and stir into the chocolate mixture until everything is completely covered.
- Tip the mixture into the lined baking tin, and spread it out to the corners.
- Sprinkle melted white chocolate and sprinkles on top
- Chill for at least 2 hrs then dust with icing sugar and cut into 12 fingers.

Egg Sponge

Prep - 15min   Cook - 15min   Serves - 6

When I learned to make this sponge, it became a family favourite in our house every Sunday. You do need an electric mixer for it as it will take forever by hand but it is worth it when served with jam and cream.

INGREDIENTS

- 3 large eggs
- 3 oz of self-raising flour
- ¼ pt whipping cream
- 3 oz castor sugar
- Strawberry jam

METHOD

- Beat the eggs and the sugar with an electric whisk until white and fluffy.
- Sieve flour and add slowly to mix folding flour into it.
- Make sure all flour is mixed well
- Grease 2 7inch sandwich tins and divide mixture into these.
- Bake at 180°C for 15 minutes until knife is clear when tested.
- Put onto to wire trays to cool
- Whisk fresh cream and spread strawberry jam on both sides and cream in the middle.
- Dust with sieved icing sugar.

Buttercream

Prep - 5min

INGREDIENTS

- 125 g butter
- 2 tbsp milk
- 1 and a half cups of icing sugar

METHOD

- Put butter into a bowl and using an electric or stand mixer let it beat for about 6 minutes until its a white colour.
- Slowly add the icing sugar until it is all blended in
- Add milk until mix is a smooth consistency
- Use to decorate an 8" birthday cake or a dozen cupcakes

Thank You!

Thank you to all the amazing children, staff, volunteers helpers and parents who we have had the pleasure to meet over the last few years at our workshops, there are too many to mention but want to especially thank Laura and Loretta from The Base @Tobin and Shauna from Sunflower support, Josie and Sinead from The Empower Project, AUsome kids, Lissan Leisure Club, The Soft Project, St Michael's GAC Lissan, Plumbridge Community Group, The Brain Injury Foundation and Anita from Health Alliance for all the help and support they have given WYSEBITES over the last few years.

To my helpers Joe, Ryan, Aloysia, Caragh, Aine, Aoife, Aoibhinn, Emma G, Susie, Amy L and Amy Mc, thank you!

A special shout out to my friends from Mums at work Network and a special mention to Sinead Norton the founder of Mums at Work who has helped me on my business journey and is an inspiration to us all!

Thank you to Padraig McAlister and his team at Innotech SWC for the help and support to create this book!
I would also like to thank Eilis Scullion for all her help with the nutrition part of my recipes.

A special mention to the students and staff I had the pleasure of working with in Holy Trinity College Cookstown, I loved every minute of it! Also to Patrick Mallon and the team in the Glenavon House Hotel for many fun years in the kitchen. I would like to thank all my family (inlaws) and friends in Dublin/Wicklow and in Northern Ireland for all the support and help they have given me over the years. A special mention to my Mum and Dad, Teresa and Tony who have been my number one supporters and my Aunts and Uncles who all loved to taste and try out my bakes and who have always encouraged me to cook.
To my sisters Evelyn, Lesley and Shaunna who always have my back and are my biggest supporters and the three amigos, Christopher Mark and Dylan who where my first guinea pigs.

WYSE BITES

(1) (Harris and Shea 2018)

(2) https://www.healthylittlefoodies.com/the-benefits-of-cooking-with-kids/#THE_BENEFITS_OF_COOKING_WITH_KIDS

(3) https://static1.squarespace.com/static/5531cbfbe4b0c759b3855d1c/t/57f6ee9d2994ca3f64322fda/1475800759698/Sensory+Food+Aversions.pdf

(4) Food refusal and avoidant eating in children including those with Autism Spectrum Conditions A practical guide for Parents and Professionals 2018 Gillian Harris and Elizabeth Shea

(5) https://www.cambridge.org/core/journals/public-health-nutrition/article/is-cooking-at-h
ome-associated-with-better-diet-quality-or-weightloss-intention/B2C8C168FFA377DD2880A217DB6AF26F

(6) https://www.qub.ac.uk/elearning/public/HealthyEating/TheEatwellPlate

(7) (healthychildren.org)2023

(8) Nutrition and Dietetic Service (2023)

(9) https://www.nhs.uk/live-well/eat-well/digestive-health/how-to-get-more-fibre-into-your
-diet

(10) https://www.wsh.nhs.uk/CMS-Documents/Patientleaflets/NutritionandDieteticService/5806-1HighFibreDietforChildren.pdf

(10.5) https://www.healthychildren.org/English/healthy-living/nutrition/Pages/Kids-Need-Fiber-Heres-Why-and-How.aspx

(11) https://www.bordbia.ie/fish/fish-for-children/

(12) www.nhs.uk/live-well/eat-well/digestive-health/how-to-get-more-fibre-into-your-diet/

(13) https://www.nidirect.gov.uk/articles/healthy-eating-children#toc-9
https://www.nhs.uk/live-well/eat-well/digestive-health/how-to-get-more-fibre-into-your-diet/

(14) https://www.nhs.uk/live-well/eat-well/food-guidelines-and-food-labels/water-drinks-nutrition/

(15) https://www.nutrition.org.uk/media/kwpd0g3o/15419-bnf-hydration-posters_children-aged-5-11-final.pdf

(16) https://www.nhsinform.scot/healthy-living/food-and-nutrition/food-safety-and-hygiene/preparing-and-cooking-food-safely

(17) https://www.bbc.co.uk/news/uk-northern-ireland-57189519

(18) https://www.autismspeaks.org/science-blog?article_type[2196]=2196&article_type[2196]=2196

(20) https://www.qub.ac.uk/News/Allnews/2023/EvidenceisbuildingtosupportawholesystemsapproachtoobesitypreventioninNorthernIreland.html

(21) Psycom.net

(22) https://autismawarenesscentre.com/constipation-witholding-and-overflow-a-deeper-dive-into-bowel-problems-for-individuals-with-asd

(23) © The Vegetarian Society carrot cake

Printed by Amazon.

The Neesons

Last but not least a special thank you to my hubby Mark and my 5 boys, Conor, Oisin, Dara, Joe and Ryan who are my WYSE BITES background Dream team and have helped me grow my business along with being my biggest critics and guinea pigs for all the recipes in this book! Thank you!

Printed in Great Britain
by Amazon